STANDING FIRM THROUGH
the GREAT
APOSTASY

STEVE GALLAGHER

BESTSELLING AUTHOR OF *At the Altar of Sexual Idolatry* AND *Intoxicated with Babylon*

STANDING FIRM THROUGH
the GREAT
APOSTASY

STEVE GALLAGHER

www.purelifeministries.org

888.PURELIFE

"The audacity of Steve Gallagher to challenge the status quo of modern-day Christianity! Leave us alone! We enjoy our sin and selfish ways. Besides, we believe that no matter how we live our salvation is guaranteed. The trouble is that Gallagher presents irrefutable evidence to the contrary. Like any good medical doctor Steve tells the Church the truth about her condition. Every page of this book cries out the question: 'What evidence do I have that I am a child of God?'"

DAVID RAVENHILL, *Author and Itinerant Teacher*

"It is rare in this day of shallow doctrine and worldliness to find someone with the courage to cry out, 'Enough!' With a heart like the prophets of old, Steve Gallagher calls God's people to godly sorrow, heart-felt repentance and renewed purity. Churches and individuals who are seeking a closer walk with God will find this book convicting and yet uplifting. I dare you to read it!"

ED BULKLEY, *Return to the Word Radio Program*

"*Standing Firm through the Great Apostasy* is very powerful and biblical. There are so many 'parrot' voices today - repeating what others say and teach. Steve's books are original and anointed. I truly feel that Steve Gallagher is a John the Baptist, calling out to today's church, as a voice crying in the wilderness, 'Make straight the way of the Lord!'"

RANDY JONES, *PRESIDENT*, *Word of Truth Ministries*

"Once again Steve Gallagher has written a book which touches a nerve in the life of the church here in America. *Standing Firm through the Great Apostasy* forces the reader to inspect his commitment to Christ and ask himself, 'Do I really know Jesus?' I highly recommend it."

RON AUCH, *Author and Pastor*

ALSO AVAILABLE BY STEVE GALLAGHER:

At the Altar of Sexual Idolatry
At the Altar of Sexual Idolatry Workbook
A Biblical Guide to Counseling the Sexual Addict
Create in Me a Pure Heart
How America Lost Her Innocence
Intoxicated with Babylon
Irresistible to God
A Lamp Unto My Feet
Living in Victory
Out of the Depths of Sexual Sin
Pressing On Toward the Heavenly Calling
The Walk of Repentance

For these books and other teaching materials please contact:

PURE LIFE MINISTRIES
14 School Street
Dry Ridge, KY 41035
(888) PURELIFE - to order
(859) 824-4444
(859) 813-0005 FAX
www.purelifeministries.org

ISBN 0-9758832-9-1
EAN 978-0-9758832-9-7

ACKNOWLEDGMENTS

Special thanks to Pastor Jim and Mari-Lee Ruddy, Pastor Eric and Michelle Hensley, Ed and Karla Buch, Pastor Cal Garcia, Chaplain Victor Marshall, Pastor Doug Detert, Rob Fisher and Dr. Ruth Ruibal for offering spiritual and doctrinal feedback on this book.

DEDICATION

To My Mother,

Thank you for teaching me true Christianity through the way you lived your life. Where would I be without your example and your prayers?

CONTENTS

INTRODUCTION

This book is an examination of a very negative and tragic subject. It is not within the scope of this book to present a balanced overview of Christianity: her strengths and weaknesses, positives and negatives, and so on. My purpose is to write about the part of the Church* that is in deep spiritual trouble. Writers of past centuries called it the Apostate Church or the Harlot Church. It is that segment of Christendom that has shown itself to be unfaithful to God.

As I extensively studied this subject in Scripture, pouring over commentaries and Bible dictionaries, a very disturbing picture began to emerge. I did my utmost to approach this subject with a sincere and honest heart. I wanted to know the truth no matter where it led me. Unfortunately, what I found was frightening and extremely upsetting. If what these men of old were saying was true, there was simply no escaping the fact that many people whom I care very deeply about are apparently heading toward hell.

One day, as I found myself becoming overwhelmed with despair, the Lord made something precious very real to me. This spiritual truth came to me in regard to my mother, Frances Gallagher.

---

* Throughout this book I will use the terms "Christian" and "Church" loosely to describe all those who profess to be evangelical believers—whether or not they actually are.

Ever since I can remember, she has gotten up long before dawn to spend time with God. Countless times during my rebellious teenage years, I would come home from a night out partying to find her sitting in her favorite rocking chair praying and reading the Bible. For 35 years she faithfully taught Sunday school to the young children of our church.

In 1990, at the age of 67, she began working as a volunteer at a local hospital. She would run errands, carry documents, deliver flowers and sometimes pray with patients. She did this in spite of the fact that, by nature, she is a shy and reticent person. She continued this volunteer work for 15 years until it became impossible for her to get to the hospital anymore. It should also be noted that for many years she sacrificially sponsored two children overseas—on top of all of her other tithes and offerings.

The revelation I received that day was that there are many like my mother in the Post-Modern Church. These "ordinary" believers simply live out the Christian life without fanfare. They are the quiet heroes of the faith. They work in offices, factories and yes, ministries. They shop at the same grocery stores, raise their kids in the same schools and usually attend the same churches. They are often unknown and "unimportant" in the Evangelical Movement.

They are *not* unknown in the hallowed halls of heaven or in the foul regions of hell.

They are the true saints of the living God. Their love for God is vibrant and contagious. Their willingness to sacrifice for the sake of others is evident to those who best know them. They are deeply consecrated to God and live with a keen awareness of the eternal realm. The Lord has His people and knows who they are, even if we often cannot discern the difference ourselves. (II Timothy 2:19)

Yes, there are a lot of tares in the field, but there is also a great deal of wheat as well. It is important to remember this as you go through this book. Otherwise you could be overcome with despair in the same way I was.

My desire is to encourage you to take a very humble and sober look at your own life. Make sure you are of the faith, beloved. Once you have sincerely settled that matter, I hope that the message contained herein will drive you to your knees for loved ones, in the same way it has me.

Section One:

THE TRUE AND FALSE CHURCH

To gain a clear understanding of the Apostate Church, we must first grasp the difference between true and false believers. There is a true Church and a false Church. There are multitudes who profess to be believers and a comparatively small number who actually are. There are those with a genuine faith in Christ and those with a dead faith.

"When Christ calls a man, he bids him come and die...because only the man who is dead to his own will can follow Christ. In fact every command of Jesus is a call to die, with all our affections and lusts."
↬ Dietrich Bonhoeffer[1]

"Christ's whole life was a Cross and Martyrdom: and thou seek rest and joy for thyself? thou art deceived..." ↬ Thomas À Kempis[2]

"The cross will cut into our lives where it hurts worst, sparing neither us nor our carefully cultivated reputations." ↬ A.W. Tozer[3]

"Those looking for the deluxe brand of salvation without a cross are more in search of salve than salvation. You can have a religion without crucifixion—but not Christianity. Life in Christ begins with the death of Self" ↬ Cecil B. Knight[4]

Chapter One:

THE MESSAGE OF THE CROSS

*Conduct yourselves in fear during the time of your
stay on earth; knowing that you were not redeemed
with perishable things...but with precious blood,
as of a lamb unblemished and spotless, the
blood of Christ. (I Peter 1:17-19)*

"What you do, do quickly." (John 13:27) With those five words, Christ set into motion the most momentous series of events the world has ever known. As the agitated Traitor hastened to finalize his rejection of the Messiah, Jesus calmly led the other disciples to the Garden of Gethsemane. What would transpire over the next several hours would shape the future of mankind. It would also establish, once and for all, what it would mean to have a relationship with God.

Jesus had much to share with His disciples that night; He had to prepare them for what was to come. His final discourse with them drew to a close as they entered the Garden. In the three and a half years these men had followed Jesus, they had never seen Him lose His composure. His deep, abiding peace remained unshakable even in the most hostile situations. But now an unmistakable change came over His countenance.

Leaving the other eight by themselves, Jesus took Peter, James and John a little further into the Garden where He "...began to be full of terror and distress..." (Mark 14:33 WNT)

"My soul is crushed with grief to the point of death," He told the favored three. (Mark 14:34 NLT) There was something so horrifying headed His way that He nearly died in the heat of the conflict.

> Then he walked forward a little way and flung himself on the ground, praying that, if it were possible, he might not have to face the ordeal. "Dear Father," he said, "all things are possible to you. Please - let me not have to drink this cup! Yet it is not what I want but what you want." (Mark 14:35-36 PHP)

"...He offered up both prayers and supplications with loud crying and tears to the One able to save Him from death..." (Hebrews 5:7) It must have broken His Father's heart to refuse such pleadings. However super-human His battle was that night, Jesus was still subject to His humanity. His anguish of soul drove Him to such an intensity of prayer that "...His sweat became like clots of blood dropping on the ground." (Luke 22:44 WNT)

What could possibly have been so appalling that Jesus would plead with His Father in such a way? The Innocent One, the Lambkin, the Darling of Heaven, was absorbing into His very being the sin of the world. In that cup was every foul crime that had ever been or would ever be committed. Is it any wonder that He shuddered at the thought of being immersed in it?

In some inexplicable way, six thousand years of sin was condensed into one horrid cupful of evil and was infused into His being. No human could comprehend the tremendous reverence and submission Jesus had to possess toward His Father for Him to utter those fateful words: "Not My will, but Thine."

No sooner had He spoken these words than Judas—now fully possessed by Satan—arrived with his treacherous kiss. Jesus passed through many hands that night, eventually landing in the custody of violent Roman soldiers. Calloused men were these Romans. Human sympathy had long since been silenced within them. They brutalized Him in a way that left Him physically mangled. "I offered my back to those who beat me and my cheeks to those who pulled out my beard. I did not hide my face from mockery and spitting." (Isaiah 50:6 NLT) They assaulted Him so savagely that He became unrecognizable. "Many people were shocked when they saw him;" wrote Isaiah. "He was so disfigured that he hardly looked human." (Isaiah 52:14 GNB)

It is very reminiscent of a tragedy that occurred a number of years ago in the West Bank of Palestine. Four Israeli soldiers inadvertently took a wrong turn and ended up in the middle of the city of Ramallah. Palestinian police arrested them, but an angry mob dragged them out of the police station. Mark Seager, a British journalist witnessed the whole event:

> I had arrived in Ramallah at about 10:30 in the morning and was getting into a taxi on the main road to go to Nablus, where there was to be a funeral that I wanted to film, when all of a sudden there came a big crowd of Palestinians shouting and running down the hill from the police station.
>
> I got out of the car to see what was happening and saw that they were dragging something behind them. Within moments they were in front of me and, to my horror, I saw that it was a body, a man they were dragging by the feet. The lower part of his body was on fire and the upper part had been shot at, and the head beaten so badly that it was a pulp, like red jelly...
>
> I thought he was a soldier because I could see the remains of khaki trousers and boots. My God, I thought, they've killed this guy. He was dead, he must have been dead, but they were still beating him, madly, kicking his head. They were like animals.

At the same time, the guy that looked like a soldier was being beaten and the crowd was getting angrier and angrier, shouting "Allah akbar" - God is great. They were dragging the dead man around the street like a cat toying with a mouse. It was the most horrible thing that I have ever seen…

It was murder of the most barbaric kind. When I think about it, I see that man's head, all smashed. I know that I'll have nightmares for the rest of my life.[5]

Jesus faced this same kind of hatred and brutality from the mob that had Him killed.

Isaiah went on to say, "We despised him and rejected him; he endured suffering and pain. No one would even look at him—we ignored him as if he were nothing." (Isaiah 53:3 GNB)

More repulsive than the physical disfigurement was the effect of taking so much evil into His being. In fact, the Apostle Paul said that He did not simply take sin upon Himself; He *became* sin itself. (II Corinthians 5:21)

It is very hard to write this, but it's possible that He was so foul to look upon that people turned away in disgust. One preacher said it this way: "He was contemptible, repulsive, loathsome and useless. He was good for nothing. When we saw Him on the Cross we said, 'Good, He deserves to die!'"[6]

Not only did man turn away from Him, but even His heavenly Father could not bear to look upon Him. God's holy nature could not be in fellowship with something so abominable. However, it is actually even worse than that. When Jesus became our sin, He was also forced to face God's wrath.

He begins to feel a foreign sensation. Somewhere during this day an unearthly foul odor began to waft, not around his nose, but his heart. He *feels* dirty. Human wickedness starts to crawl upon his spotless being—the living excrement from our souls. The apple of his Father's eye turns brown with rot.

His Father! He must face his Father like this!

From heaven the Father now rouses himself like a lion disturbed, shakes his mane, and roars against the shriveling remnant of a man hanging on a cross. *Never* has the Son seen the Father look at him so, never felt even the least of his hot breath. But the roar shakes the unseen world and darkens the visible sky. The Son does not recognize these eyes.[7]

Somehow the prophet had seen this transpire some 700 years before. "Yet we ourselves esteemed Him stricken, smitten of God, and afflicted. But He was pierced through for our transgressions, He was crushed for our iniquities; the chastening for our well-being fell upon Him…" (Isaiah 53:4b-5) One can only imagine what Jesus faced during those three hours of darkness that He hung on that Cross alone. "My God, My God, why have You forsaken Me?" He cried. (Matthew 27:46 NKJV)

It would probably serve every Christian well to somberly consider how it must have affected God to hear His beloved Son cry out like that. Perhaps that is why, when he spoke of the price that was paid for our redemption, Peter solemnly instructed us to conduct ourselves in fear. (I Peter 1:17-19) It also helps to explain the fearful implication found in the following warning given by the writer of Hebrews:

> Dear friends, if we deliberately continue sinning after we have received knowledge of the truth, there is no longer any sacrifice that will cover these sins. There is only the terrible expectation of God's judgment and the raging fire that will consume his enemies…
>
> Just think how much worse the punishment will

be for those who have trampled on the Son of God, and have treated the blood of the covenant, which made us holy, as if it were common and unholy, and have insulted and disdained the Holy Spirit who brings God's mercy to us.

For we know the one who said, "I will take revenge. I will pay them back." He also said, "The LORD will judge his own people." It is a terrible thing to fall into the hands of the living God. (Hebrews 10:26-31 NLT)

Those who treat the Blood of Christ with a flippant attitude may well be doing so to their own destruction.

THE MESSAGE OF THE CROSS

For some time Jesus had understood that He would have to face the Cross. Just before leaving Galilee for the final time, He told His disciples, "The Son of Man must suffer many things and be rejected by the elders and chief priests and scribes, and be killed…" (Luke 9:22)

Suffer many things? Be rejected? Be killed? How would these simple men respond to this alarming information? Peter, full of sentimental mercy and fearful about what it would mean to him personally, rebuked his Master: "God forbid it, Lord! This shall never happen to You." (Matthew 16:22) Jesus immediately reproved him: "Get behind Me, Satan! You are a stumbling block to Me; for you are not setting your mind on God's interests, but man's." (Matthew 16:23)

While Peter and the other ten recoiled at the implication of Jesus' prediction, their devotion to Him had long since been decided. These men would spend the rest of their time on earth laying down their lives for His sake. Judas, on the other hand, wanted no part in such a life and these words only confirmed a resolution that had been growing within him for some time.

George Bowen captures the difference between Judas and the other disciples.

> There was love to Christ in the eleven—most immature, a mere germ, a love ill-prepared to stand the fiery trial to which it was about to be subjected, yet nevertheless a genuine beginning of love destined ere long to triumph over all opposition. But there was not this in Judas. He loved not Christ. Something or other in the character or in the work of Christ had attracted him but as the character of Christ became more unveiled to him, he experienced more and more of repugnancy. He preferred himself, with all his sins, all his vileness, to the Son of God. The [selflessness] and spirit of sacrifice conspicuous in Christ awoke no fellow-response in him, but on the contrary jarred strongly on his feelings. The words, the acts, the looks, that drew the other disciples to their Master, only served to widen the gulf betwixt him and the Savior.[8]

What Judas, in his carnal thinking, could not comprehend was that the Messiah had to die to accomplish God's great work for His life. His impending death on the Cross would make a way for people of all ages to be redeemed from the power of sin and enter the kingdom of heaven. There would be only one avenue into the land of glory and it would go straight through Calvary. Because of what was accomplished there by the Messiah, the intricate demands of the Law—which were *Self*-dependent—were no longer necessary for salvation.

Now, a man would only need to repent of his rebellion to God's commandments and entrust his life to Christ. The Cross would forever stand as an impenetrable barrier for any who would attempt to enter heaven through any other means.

Calvary represents God's great love for mankind—a jealous love, a love that expects reciprocal affection. It was never meant to be a "free pass" to live in disobedience or Self-will. It actually meant the exact opposite. Those who decided to follow Jesus would be recognized by distinct similarities to His life and death. The life of Judas represents those of all ages who desire the heaven of Christ without the Cross of Christ.

After warning the Twelve about what would happen in Jerusalem, Jesus gave a small talk that was considered so important by the gospel writers that all four of them included it in their books.* Jesus made it clear that what He expressed in this talk would forevermore delineate the true from the false Christian: "If anyone wishes to come after Me, he must deny himself, and take up his cross and follow Me." (Matthew 16:24) In this succinct statement, Jesus offers three requirements to being His follower.

YOU MUST DENY SELF

Scripture makes it clear that there is no salvation apart from repentance. (Mark 1:15) It should be noted as well that a person cannot repent unless there is some acknowledgement of actual guilt. And a person's guilt cannot be properly comprehended without understanding the judicial aspect of salvation. Unfortunately, a terribly erroneous view of this process has been propagated within the Church. The correct and incorrect views of the repentance that leads to salvation can be better understood by considering the following two courtroom scenarios.

Scenario One

James stands in the criminal docket of the high court, charged with treason against God's kingdom. The devil acts as the man's accuser before God. Jesus is the defense attorney who takes up his cause. "Your Honor," Jesus says, "what the devil

---

* I can think of no other teaching Jesus gave about which this can be said.

says about James is a total exaggeration! Yes, he's made some mistakes and hasn't always been the man he should have been, but in his heart of hearts he's a good man. I will take whatever sins he has committed upon Myself!" Hearing that, the Judge dismisses all charges against the defendant.

Scenario Two

William stands in the criminal docket of the high court, charged with treason against God's kingdom. It is not the devil but the Holy Spirit, Scripture and his own conscience that act as his accusers.† A long line of witnesses step forth to testify about the many times he disobeyed God and acted in Self-will. Over and over again specific deeds of treachery are recalled.

When all of the evidence has been presented, it is the man himself who steps forward to speak. "Your Honor, not the half of my crimes against You have been told. I am guilty as charged! I know that I deserve the full penalty of the Law, but I am asking for mercy. If You will give me another opportunity, I promise to do my utmost to live the rest of my life adhering to Your law." Hearing this, Jesus steps forward and offers to pay the penitent man's sentence. The Judge immediately dismisses all charges against the defendant.

Notice the different perspectives offered in these two scenarios. James' guilt is presented in very general terms. Yes, he knows he is a sinner, but the concept is very vague. His attitude is tantamount to a leper dismissing the blotch that has appeared on his arm as a superficial blemish. The pangs of guilt that plague him are dismissed as an attack of the devil. Jesus is viewed as his defender. It is this concept of God's grace that unbroken, unrepentant Christians gravitate toward.

Notice the difference in William's attitude. He solemnly

---

† Satan is called the accuser of the brethren, not the accuser of sinners. (Revelation 12:10) If anything, the devil will do his utmost to encourage a sinner to minimize his sin, justify himself or seek some other way to shift the blame off himself.

reviews his life and examines his heart. His final verdict about himself is that he is terribly guilty. Instead of Jesus deserving to hang on the Cross, he sees himself as belonging there. He would consider the words of the preacher quoted previously about the dying Jesus as being appropriately spoken to himself: "You are contemptible, repulsive, loathsome and useless. You are good for nothing...You deserve to die!"

This is what it means to deny Self. A person cannot and will not follow Christ until he has renounced his allegiance to Self.‡ As long as Self reigns in his heart, as long as he is primarily devoted to Self, he will repeatedly prove himself to be a traitor to Christ's kingdom. The atrociousness of Judas' crime had more to do with the fact that he knew the Savior intimately and still rejected His authority than it did with his actual betrayal.

The doctrine of the depravity of man is little more than a nebulous teaching to people like James because they are determined to see themselves in the most positive light. They want to see themselves as good people and are unwilling to acknowledge that they are intrinsically evil. Most of them are buoyed in this sanguine viewpoint by the fact that they have been able to avoid involvement in flagrant sin such as fornication, drug abuse and so on. Seeing themselves as being inherently good means they do not need a Savior; therefore they will not have one.

It is very interesting that the very people who consider themselves as being vastly superior to a man like Judas are usually the ones who most resemble him spiritually. I say this because, like Judas, pseudo-Christians have never come to grips with their own wickedness, never truly repented of their sins and thus, have never been converted to Christ.

They love to censure people like Judas, Adolph Hitler or Charles Manson because it strengthens their conviction about

---

‡ It should be noted that some believers come to this point over time. Not everyone has the kind of dramatic conversion that instantly transfers the allegiance of his heart to God. However, if it has been a true conversion, that allegiance will shift over time.

their own goodness. This underlying belief in the quality of one's character is the very thing which minimizes sin, avoids examining one's heart and fends off the conviction of the Holy Spirit. In short, the desire to see oneself favorably is what keeps people from experiencing the kind of true repentance that brings forth a transformed character.

The reason that unconverted churchgoers can sidestep the truth about themselves is that the human heart is an inveterate liar. It truly is "deceitful above all things." (Jeremiah 17:9) If a person were to catch an acquaintance in an outright lie once or twice, he would never again trust anything the person might tell him. How amazing then is the level of trust people have for their own hearts—in spite of the fact that they have repeatedly caught the wretch fabricating the truth. Nevertheless, those who *want to be flattered* will return to this polluted well for facts about themselves time and again. They return because they are told what they want to hear.

Nothing hinders an honest self-evaluation like self-flattery. The reason people like James become terribly offended when they are encouraged to make sure they are in the faith is because they view it as an attack upon their character. They think that they are saved because they are "good people." They do not understand that hell holds multitudes of people who are humanly good. But heaven is not for good people; it is for sinners who have truly repented. Hell is for rebels who will not repent.

The very ones who are in most need of questioning their faith are, tragically, the ones who are least likely to do so. False Christians are often those who feel the most eternally secure. As George Bowen said, "The faith that does not hearken to Christ, that hearkens rather to one's own heart, is a mere phantom faith; it is the demon of unbelief under the angelic mask of faith."[9]

When Jesus tells His followers they must deny themselves, He is saying that they must give up the false notion that they deserve salvation. They must point their finger at Self and exclaim, "He is guilty and deserves to die!"

YOU MUST TAKE UP YOUR CROSS

Not only must there be an initial renunciation of Self, but there must be an ongoing rejection of its claims upon the believer's life. But how can a person turn away from the incessant demands that well up from within his own being? Herein lies the essential difference between the true and false convert.

The unconverted churchgoer can initiate certain religious observances into his life, but his best efforts will soon exhaust themselves. (Romans 8:7-8)

The reason many Christians cringe when they are asked to sacrifice for the sake of others is that nothing has happened within them to compel them to get outside of themselves. They see carrying a cross as an uninvited intrusion upon their lives. In their heart of hearts, their true devotion is reserved for the world system that caters to their flesh.

On the other hand, the person who has come to grips with his lost condition and has truly been redeemed lives with an overwhelming sense of gratitude toward his Savior. When Jesus tells him that He has fashioned a special cross just for him, he sees it as a joy and privilege. "You want to use *me*? You consider *me* as being worthy to serve in Your kingdom?"

Although many see picking up a cross in a negative light, Paul counted it to be a hallmark of true Christianity. He wrote, "God has made us what we are, and in our union with Christ Jesus he has created us for a life of good deeds, which he has already prepared for us to do." (Ephesians 2:10 GNB) This is not a life of drudgery but of the greatest joy for a believer!

The unavoidable truth is that not everyone who considers himself to be a Christian truly is one. Conversion occurs when the person makes a decision deep within to transfer his allegiance to God's kingdom. It is as if Pilate stands at his heart and says, "Behold the Man! Shall I crucify Christ or the Barabbas of *Self* dwelling in your bosom?" One or the other must be allowed to live; the other must be put to death. The implications of this decision are eternal.

The fundamental difference between a true and false believer lies in the question of loyalty. Is he devoted to Christ or to himself? When it comes right down to it, is he going to look out for "number one" or will his primary loyalties be to Christ? Will he do his own will or that of God? Will he love Self or will he love the Lord? Being born again means the person is converted from a Self-centered existence to one which is becoming increasingly Christ-centered.

The message of the Cross is diametrically opposed to loyalty to Self. Jesus says, "You are not to believe in yourself; you are to believe in Me. You are not to love yourself; you are to love God. You are not to be stingy with yourself; you are to give yourself away for the sake of others. In short, you are to deny yourself."

This message is what turned the heart of Judas because, when it came right down to it, he was unwilling to renounce Self and he was unwilling to take up his cross.

YOU MUST FOLLOW ME

The entire life of Jesus was aimed in one direction: the Cross. As much as soothsayers may attempt to paint it in a different light, Scripture offers no illusions to mask the difficult road of Christianity. As the Apostle Paul once grimly stated, "Through many tribulations we must enter the kingdom of God." (Acts 14:22) No matter how rugged and perilous this path may be, true believers will always be found there because, to them, the alternative is unthinkable.

On the other hand, unconverted Christians have no

intention of going down that road. Their solution is to simply create another gospel that will allow Self to retain control of their lives. They too are on a path, but it is headed in a different direction.

Paul fully understood that there were two separate roads available to those who considered themselves to be Christians. He told the Corinthians, "The word of the cross is foolishness to those who are perishing, but to us who are being saved it is the power of God." (I Corinthians 1:18) This declaration established once and for all the difference between the competing mindsets of living for Self or living for Christ. It would be worthwhile to make a few observations about this statement.

Notice first of all that everyone who hears the "word of the cross" is included in these two groups. A person's attitude to the preaching of the Cross is said to be the determining factor as to which direction he is headed. Once the Holy Spirit makes real the words of Jesus, the person will either enter the process of becoming conformed into the image of Christ or he will grow increasingly more hard-hearted toward the things of God. The difference may be imperceptible at first. Jesus was the only one who could discern the difference in the hearts of Judas and Peter; wheat and tares look identical in their early stages.

Notice also that the grammar makes plain the fact that salvation and damnation are both ongoing processes. These are pathways on which every professing Christian—every hearer of the word of the Cross—is traveling.

Those who embrace the message of the Cross are in the process of being saved. Elsewhere Paul speaks of salvation being past tense (Romans 8:24), present tense (I Corinthians 15:2) and future tense (Romans 10:9). Day by day they are becoming more saved than before: "...the path of the righteous is like the light of dawn, that shines brighter and brighter until the full day." (Proverbs 4:18)

On the other hand, having a disdain for Jesus' words is a

sure sign that a person is in a perishing condition. As Alexander MacLaren once said, "And if to us the Cross is 'foolishness,' it is because already a process of 'perishing' has gone so far that it has attacked our capacity of recognizing the wisdom and love of God when we see them."[10]

Paul employed the word *foolishness* (Gk. *moria*) again in the following chapter: "But a natural man does not accept the things of the Spirit of God, for they are foolishness to him; and he cannot understand them, because they are spiritually appraised." (I Corinthians 2:14) The very fact that a person shuns the word of the Cross is proof that he does not have the Spirit of God indwelling him.

Such people do not want to deny Self; they want to live for Self. They do not want to say *no* to the flesh; they want to say *yes* to it. They do not want to pick up their cross; they want to avoid it.

Those who reject the Cross may have become more knowledgeable about spiritual matters over the years, but it has not translated into a more godly life. They claim to be His followers, but they do not really desire to go where He is going. They are headed in a completely different direction. Where did they get the idea that they could live for Self, disdain the Cross and still claim to be followers of Christ?

It is clear that they are not being honest with themselves. Their Christianity is outward and has not penetrated their hearts. The painful truth is they are false converts.

"The only saving faith is that which casts itself on God for life or death." ⮞ Martin Luther[1]

"I doubt if five percent of professing Christians are born again." ⮞ Leonard Ravenhill[2]

"We can see both the true Church, the bride of Christ, as well as the false church of harlotry. The latter has no understanding of God's laws; therefore, she has no fear of God. She walks in darkness, death and destruction."
⮞ Milton Green[3]

"Never having had a true sense of sin, they nevertheless experienced some alarms, and they set down those alarms for repentance. Although they have never truly believed in the Lord Jesus, they have felt a degree of peace, and have come to look upon this treacherous calm as the result of true faith. They have never really received a new heart, still there is a measure of reformation, and they mistake the outward for the inward." ⮞ Charles Spurgeon[4]

Chapter Two:

THE MEANING OF THE PARABLES

*"Then Jesus asked them, 'Don't you understand
this parable? How, then, will you ever understand
any parable?'" (Mark 4:13 GNB)*

Christianity begins and ends in the heart. This statement
is true because the heart is the seedbed where ideas are
formed, attitudes developed and out of which thoughts
spring forth. It is the essence of man's being. As such, it is also
the home of the will—that mysterious function of the human
heart which makes the decisions that determine a person's
eternal destiny. Solomon said that God "set eternity in [man's]
heart." (Ecclesiastes 3:11) Jesus later said, "...the kingdom of God
is within you." (Luke 17:21 KJV)

No wonder the Lord exclaimed, "Oh that they had such
a heart in them, that they would fear Me, and keep all My
commandments always, that it may be well with them and with
their sons forever!" (Deuteronomy 5:29)

Because the reality of a person's spiritual condition is buried
so deeply within him and is visible only with divine discernment,
it is possible for him to act as though he has a relationship to
the Lord which he doesn't actually possess. It was this tendency
to settle for a superficial and outward relationship that caused

Jehovah to lament, "…this people draw near with their words and honor Me with their lip service, but they remove their hearts far from Me, and their reverence for Me consists of tradition learned by rote." (Isaiah 29:13)

The message of the parables (that relate to the kingdom of God) is that the Church contains both sincere believers and those who have never actually crossed the line into a submissive relationship with God. Pseudo-Christians have made outward alterations to their lives, but in their hearts, they remain unconverted.

The parables Jesus gave about the Kingdom are primarily found in Matthew 13. The opening allegory is the Sower and the Seed, which seems to play the primary role in relating the main truth that Jesus was conveying. Indeed, its importance can be seen in the fact that it is included in all three synoptic gospels. Ray Comfort writes the following about its message:

> The fact that there are true and false conversions is made very clear in the statement Jesus made to His disciples in Mark 4:13. He had just given them the parable of the sower, and the disciples asked what He meant by it: "And He said to them, 'Do you not understand this parable? How then will you understand all parables?'" *In other words, the parable of the sower is the key to unlocking the mysteries of all the other parables.*
>
> Once that understanding has been established, then the light of perception begins to dawn on the rest of what Jesus said in parables about the Kingdom of God. In fact, if someone doesn't understand the principle of the true and false being alongside each other, they will be in the dark about almost everything Jesus taught, because He taught in parables…[5]

The Sower and the Seed

The opening parable Jesus shares provides a clear picture of what transpires within a person's heart when the Word of truth is presented to him. Certain aspects of the story are obvious. The seed is the flawless Word of God. Jesus later said that His words "...are spirit and are life." (John 6:63) The written Word, just like His spoken word, has the divine efficacy to go into the soil of a person's heart and bring forth life. It is simply a law of nature that if you put a seed in good soil and add moisture, it will grow into a healthy plant and, in time, produce fruit after its own kind.

The Sower is the Holy Spirit. The picture here is a farmer indiscriminately throwing seed throughout a vast field. The only variable presented in this parable is the different types of soil—each representing the hearts of those who are presented the truths of the gospel. Each of the soils mentioned represents a different class of hearers.

The superficial reader will tend to interpret these different people groups from an outward perspective. Again, I must stress that everything spiritual that occurs in a person's life begins in the heart. To properly understand the response from these four different types of people requires us to examine what transpires *within* them.

> Those along the traveled road are the people who have heard; then the devil comes and carries away the message out of their hearts, that they may not believe (acknowledge Me as their Savior and devote themselves to Me) and be saved [here and hereafter]. (Luke 8:12 AMP)

The first heart presented is illustrated through the picture of seed which "...fell beside the road, and the birds came and ate them up." (Matthew 13:4) Jesus interprets it as saying, "When anyone hears the word of the kingdom and does not understand it, the evil one comes and snatches away what has been sown in his heart." (Matthew 13:19) Luke adds, "so that they will not believe and be saved." (Luke 8:12)*

This describes the person who has grown cold to the truths of Scripture. There was a time when he was interested in the Kingdom, but when it came right down to it, he was unwilling to lay his heart on the altar and submit his life to Christ.

Instead of earnestly responding to the Word when it was presented to him over the years, this person would let it slip by. Time and again the Holy Spirit would convict him about his refusal to surrender his life to God, but he successfully warded off every attempt to reach him. Over time, familiarity with truth caused a deep cynicism to take root within him. The Bible seemed to grow increasingly more stale to his unresponsive heart: "every statement, every appeal, every remonstrance, every warning, is an old familiar sound, 'a twice-told tale.'"[6]

"His soul is not deeply convinced of its guilt and depravity," writes Adam Clarke; "the fallow ground is not properly ploughed up, nor the rock broken."[7] Matthew Henry says that, "Hypocrites…are told of free salvation, of the believer's privileges, and the happiness of heaven; and, without any change of heart, without any abiding conviction of their own depravity, their need of a Saviour, or the excellence of holiness, they soon profess an unwarranted assurance."[8]

Every time he would be subjected to Scripture, the ever

---

* Perhaps this would be a good opportunity to explain why the teachings of Jesus often vary from one gospel writer to another. I think I can satisfactorily answer this question from my own experience as a preacher. I have given certain messages dozens of times. In one situation, I might use an illustration slightly differently than on another occasion. Also, what stands out to one listener might be different than what another heard. Matthew was a first-hand witness of the teachings and events of Jesus. Mark recorded what Peter recounted to him. Luke was a Greek historian who interviewed witnesses several decades after these things actually occurred. Thus, the differences in the gospel accounts should not be taken as contradictory but should be seen as complementary depictions of the life and teachings of Christ.

watchful agents of Satan were quick to snatch it away by redirecting his attention to some trivial interest. His lack of true concern over spiritual matters made him an easy target for the foul birds of hell.

Yes, he may be careful to obey biblical commandments about obvious sins, but he has been content to hold a shallow viewpoint of the Christian faith. He is blind to the fact that his life is full of biblical inconsistencies.

Over time, the hard-baked clay of his heart became impenetrable to the Word of God. "Unbelief makes us practical atheists," wrote Joel Beeke. "Hell is no longer hell, heaven is no longer heaven, grace is no longer grace, sin is no longer sin, Christ is no longer Christ, God is no longer God, and the Bible is no longer the everlasting Word of God."[9] This terrible hardening effect of unbelief hinders the person's heart from responding sincerely to the Word. This person should have heeded the warning given in the book of Hebrews: "Today if you hear His voice, do not harden your hearts..." (Hebrews 3:15)

> As for what was sown on thin (rocky) soil, this is he who hears the Word and at once welcomes and accepts it with joy; Yet it has no real root in him, but is temporary (inconstant, lasts but a little while); and when affliction or trouble or persecution comes on account of the Word, at once he is caused to stumble [he is repelled and begins to distrust and desert Him Whom he ought to trust and obey] and he falls away. (Matthew 13:20-21 AMP)

The soil of the second person is described as "rocky." The seed of faith actually sprouted forth with promise, but "...as soon as it grew up, it withered away, because it had no moisture." (Luke 8:6) Matthew further explains that the person has "...no depth of soil." (Matthew 13:5) Jesus says these people are "those who, when they hear, receive the word with joy; and these have no firm root; they believe for a while, and in time of temptation fall away." (Luke 8:13) Matthew adds that their faith is only "temporary." (Matthew 13:21)

Initially this person responded to the Truth with enthusiasm. Unlike the person of hardened soil, he is quite willing to surrender his life to God. He throws himself into Christianity without reserve. His enthusiasm seems to indicate a powerful conversion. Perhaps he was "led to the Lord" by someone who shared all of the benefits of Christianity without mentioning the cross he must bear. (Matthew 16:24)

In any case, it is only a matter of time before the Lord allows the genuineness of his faith to be tested. In regards to this essential aspect of the salvation process, Peter would later exclaim, "In this you greatly rejoice, even though now for a little while, if necessary, you have been distressed by various trials, so that the proof of your faith, being more precious than gold which is perishable, even though tested by fire, may be found to result in praise and glory and honor at the revelation of Jesus Christ." (I Peter 1:6-7)

The value of the testing process will not be fully realized until the hereafter, but Scripture is very clear about its necessity. However, this is the point of departure for this group of people. They're happy to be Christians as long as it doesn't cost them anything they consider valuable. If these shallow natures can be assured a place in heaven by going to church and abstaining from a few outward sins, they're happy to be followers of Christ. But as soon as Jesus begins to reveal to them that they have a cross to bear in life, their interest wanes. The Pulpit Commentary says this:

> Underneath that outside of seeming life there lay the heart unchanged, unconverted, hard and cold as rock...they have not counted the cost; they have looked only on the fair side of religion, not on its severer aspect.

They have never thought deeply of the sharpness of the cross, of their own danger, of the sacrifices which the cross demands. That premature joy is often a bad sign; it often means that there is no sense of sin, no genuine sorrow and contrition for the past.[10]

Once these people realize the price involved with true Christianity, they quickly begin to back peddle in their hearts. The decision to fall away from the faith is made deep within. The more honest ones quit going to church altogether. Others simply convince themselves that they don't have to be "fanatics." They tell themselves that they love the Lord, but the truth is that they love their lives in this world. They maintain the outward life of a Christian but are unwilling to follow Christ to Calvary. As Ray Comfort writes, "An even greater tragedy than people falling away from the Church is the fact that multitudes of unrepentant 'believers' stay within its midst. These people rest in their 'conversion experience…' and will do so until they cry, 'Lord, Lord.'"[11]

And the ones sown among the thorns are others who hear the Word; then the cares and anxieties of the world and distractions of the age, and the pleasure and delight and false glamour and deceitfulness of riches, and the craving and passionate desire for other things creep in and choke and suffocate the Word, and it becomes fruitless. (Mark 4:18-19 AMP)

The third group of people are illustrated by the seed which "…fell among the thorns; and the thorns grew up with it and choked it out." (Luke 8:8) Mark adds that "…it yielded no crop." (Mark 4:7) In this case we find soil rich enough to promise a hardy crop. However, this person's soil wasn't properly prepared.

These people receive the Word "…but the worries of the

world, and the deceitfulness of riches, and the desires for other things enter in and choke the word, and it becomes unfruitful." (Mark 4:19) Luke adds that "...they are choked with worries and riches and pleasures of this life, and bring no fruit to maturity." (Luke 8:14)

The picture here is of a person with a seedling of faith alive within his innermost being, but little by little, the thorns of worldly interests and idols are allowed to resurface in his life. Mark's version breaks down the problem into three separate categories: the worries of the world, the deceitfulness of riches, and the desires for other things.

In today's hectic world especially, if a Christian doesn't take great care to prevent it, he can easily become driven by an unrelenting concern over the mundane issues of the daily life. It is very easy for a person's spiritual life to be swallowed up by the distractions of taking care of the business of life. The sincere believer will fight for his spiritual life and will not allow God to be crowded out of his heart. Earlier Jesus had said, "You cannot serve both God and money. That is why I tell you not to worry about everyday life... These things dominate the thoughts of unbelievers, but your heavenly Father already knows all your needs." (Matthew 6:24-32 NLT)

In a similar way, living in a prosperous nation can make a careless Christian extremely vulnerable to the seducing pull of success. It is very easy to justify throwing oneself into work. Men are especially vulnerable to this worldly allurement. Indeed, many ministers deceive themselves into thinking they are laboring for souls when actually they are addicted to acquiring all of the benefits of outward success.

The last category describes a person's lust for all of the various types of pleasure, entertainment and attractions this world offers. My book, *Intoxicated with Babylon*, is an in-depth study of how the spirit of this world has seduced believers away from a genuine life in God:

The world has a thousand charms to lure the
believer away from a vibrant, genuine love relationship
with God...

These three carnal appetites, the lust of the flesh, the
lust of the eyes, and the lust of pride, are branches of sin.
The lust of the flesh represents the entire realm of pleasure,
entertainment, amusement, and comfort, and includes
addictions, movies, sports, television, travel, and all the
many kinds of activities people become involved in. The
lust of the eyes describes a person's intense desire to have
something he sees. It usually revolves around the desire for
possessions: trendy clothes, the latest technology, a new
car, and so on. The pride of life is a person's exaggerated
estimate of his own value as a person. Self-ambition, a
drive to be successful, to have more prominence, an urge
to "keep up with the Joneses," or the prideful desire to "be
the one"—these are the evidences of the pride of life.[12]

Most of the interests mentioned above are innocuous in
themselves. The problem is that Christians allow them to absorb
their minds to such an extent that their ability to connect with
God in a meaningful way is lost. They too continue to live the
outward life of a believer, but the reality of their heart shows
that they have forfeited their love for God in favor of their
beloved worldly interests.

The final epitaph of this person's life could be summed up
thus: "He might have been a saint of God; but, alas! he hath
gained the world, he hath lost his soul."[13]

And those sown on the good (well-adapted) soil are
the ones who hear the Word and receive and accept and
welcome it and bear fruit—some thirty times as much
as was sown, some sixty times as much, and some [even]
a hundred times as much. (Mark 4:20 AMP)

Lastly, Jesus spoke of those who "...hear the word and accept it and bear fruit, thirty, sixty, and a hundredfold." (Mark 4:20) Luke offers profound insight when he quotes Jesus as saying that these people "...heard the word in an honest and good heart, and hold it fast, and bear fruit with perseverance." (Luke 8:15)

The fact that this person has "an honest (Gk. *kalos*) and good (Gk. *agathos*) heart" would explain why he is willing to "accept it." One Bible version translates it as "open minds and in a right spirit."[14]

Actually, both of these words (*kalos* and *agathos*) are nearly always translated as *good*. So, the literal translation would be that this person has "a good and good heart." Vine describes the subtle difference between the two: "*Kalos* denotes that which is intrinsically good, and so, goodly, fair, beautiful...*Agathos* describes that which, being good in its character or constitution, is beneficial in its effect."[15]

Jesus is not refuting earlier statements that man's heart is "desperately wicked" (Jeremiah 17:9) and is the source of evil thoughts and behaviors. (Mark 7:21-23) The point He is making here is simply that some people have a sincere willingness to hear and respond to the Truth. Once again Jesus alludes to the fact that there are true and false believers.

A true believer always bears fruit. Consider some of the ways these Greek terms (*kalos* and *agathos*) are employed regarding fruit:

- The axe is already laid at the root of the trees; therefore every tree that does not bear good (*kalos*) fruit is cut down and thrown into the fire. (Matthew 3:10)
- So every good (*agathos*) tree bears good (*kalos*) fruit, but the bad tree bears bad fruit. (Matthew 7:17)
- Every tree that does not bear good (*kalos*) fruit is cut down and thrown into the fire. (Matthew 7:19)
- Either make the tree good (*kalos*) and its fruit good

(*kalos*), or make the tree bad and its fruit bad; for the tree is known by its fruit. (Matthew 12:13)

Indeed, Jesus describes the person with good soil as bearing fruit: "some a hundredfold, some sixty, and some thirty." Obviously, the veracity of a person's faith is proven in the fact that he bears fruit.

THE OTHER KINGDOM PARABLES

Upon concluding His first parable, Jesus immediately offers another one: the Parable of the Wheat and Tares. Here is the explanation of this parable which Jesus offered to His inquisitive disciples:

> The one who sows the good seed is the Son of Man, and the field is the world; and as for the good seed, these are the sons of the kingdom; and the tares are the sons of the evil one; and the enemy who sowed them is the devil, and the harvest is the end of the age; and the reapers are angels.
> So just as the tares are gathered up and burned with fire, so shall it be at the end of the age. The Son of Man will send forth His angels, and they will gather out of His kingdom all stumbling blocks, and those who commit lawlessness, and will throw them into the furnace of fire; in that place there will be weeping and gnashing of teeth. Then the righteous will shine forth as the sun in the kingdom of their Father. He who has ears, let him hear. (Matthew 13:37-42)

Jesus seems intent on pressing home the fact that not everyone who claims to be His follower truly is. The two-fold point made in this parable is that there will always be a mixture of true and false believers in the Church *on earth* and that this cannot be rectified by rash attempts to purify it.[†] Further support for this perspective of the meaning of the parables can be found in the nearly unanimous comments of reputable commentators. For instance, the following is what a few said regarding the identity of the tares:

"Thus, 'tares' aptly represented hypocrites in the church. Strongly resembling Christians in their experience, and, in some respects, their lives it is impossible to distinguish them from genuine Christians…Our Saviour teaches us here that hypocrites and deceived persons must be expected in the church."[16] Albert Barnes

"This parable represents the present and future state of the gospel church; Christ's care of it, the devil's enmity against it, the mixture there is in it of good and bad in this world…"[17] Matthew Henry

"The righteous and the wicked are often mingled in the visible Church…It is the interest of Satan to introduce hypocrites and wicked persons into religious societies, in order to discredit the work of God, and to favor his own designs."[18] Adam Clarke

"…nominal Christians, and fair moralists, but who know nothing of the life of God."[19] Charles Spurgeon

This parable is followed up a few verses later by yet another that once again reinforces the message:

---

† It should be noted here that Scripture lays down clear guidelines as to dealing with ungodly persons within the local church: Matthew 18:15-17; I Corinthians 5:11; II Timothy 3:5; Titus 3:10; II John 1:10.

Again, the kingdom of heaven is like a dragnet cast
into the sea, and gathering fish of every kind; and when
it was filled, they drew it up on the beach; and they sat
down and gathered the good fish into containers, but
the bad they threw away. So it will be at the end of the
age; the angels will come forth and take out the wicked
from among the righteous, and will throw them into the
furnace of fire; in that place there will be weeping and
gnashing of teeth. (Matthew 13:47-50)

Once again, Jesus is warning His listeners about the fact
that there would be many people who were part of the crowd
who followed Him but were nevertheless not true converts.
Again, I will turn to the writings of others to state what should
be obvious to all:

By the net may be understood the preaching of the
Gospel of the kingdom, which keeps drawing men into
the profession of Christianity, and into the fellowship of
the visible Church of Christ...By picking out the good,
and throwing away the bad, is meant that separation
which God shall make between false and true professors,
casting the former into hell, and bringing the latter to
heaven.[20] Adam Clarke

To be in the kingdom is not enough; some of those
now within it may nevertheless be cast out. It thus greatly
resembles the parable of the ten virgins; save that in that
parable greater stress is laid on personal preparation and
continued watchfulness; in this, on personal worth.[21]
Pulpit Commentary

Notice the good fish and the bad fish were in the
net together. The world is not caught in the dragnet

of the Kingdom of Heaven; they remain in the world. The "fish" who are caught, are those who respond to the Gospel—the evangelical "catch." Then the good (true converts) and the bad (false converts) remain side by side within the net of the Church until the time of judgment.

The parables Jesus gave are full of references to the spurious convert. For instance—Matthew 22:10, "Those slaves went out into the streets and gathered together all they found, both evil and good; and the wedding hall was filled with dinner guests."

This was the story of the man without a wedding garment. Notice again the "bad" were "gathered" with the good—the true and the false. This man was someone the servants had brought in from the highways for the marriage feast. He had obviously been gathered evangelically. He thought he was a guest within the Kingdom of God, but he was not; and his error was that he did not have a robe of righteousness, and was therefore never a Christian.[22] Ray Comfort

After telling this story about the man without a wedding garment, Jesus said, "For many are called, but few are chosen." (Matthew 22:14) In other words, there are many plants in the field, but only a few are actually wheat; there are many fish in the net, but only a few are true converts. The few have been chosen because they were truly converted to Christ and remained faithful to Him.

And finally, Jesus expresses what a true conversion looks like by offering these two adjoining parables.

The kingdom of heaven is like a treasure hidden in the field, which a man found and hid again; and from joy over it he goes and sells all that he has and buys that field.

> Again, the kingdom of heaven is like a merchant seeking fine pearls, and upon finding one pearl of great value, he went and sold all that he had and bought it. (Matthew 13:44-46)

These two parables are simply stating in another form what the other parables have stated. The obvious point Jesus is making is that when a person truly becomes born again, the benefits of his salvation mean everything to him. No sacrifice is too great for the true convert. George Bowen writes: "It may be well to examine yourself and see what effect the unparalleled exhibition of love and mercy in the Gospel has had upon you. You are sitting at a banquet of promises, each of them worth more than ten thousand talents; you, that should be lifting up your eyes in torment, are sitting at the table of the Lord of life…Now, what is the effect of it all upon you?"[23]

The point to the parable of the Pearl of Great Price is that someone who has a true conversion brings forth fruit because he realizes what has happened for him. The unspoken inference that can be derived in this parable about the false believer is that he does not bring forth fruit because he has never really been to the Cross.

The message of the parables of Matthew 13 is that there are both true and false Christians in the world. Just because a person has had some spiritual experiences and attends a Bible-believing church does not necessarily mean that he has truly entered the Kingdom of God.

The entrance to that kingdom comes only through a genuine conversion.

"Christ says, 'Give me All. I don't want so much of your time and so much of your money and so much of your work: I want You. I have not come to torment your natural self, but to kill it...I will give you a new self instead. In fact, I will give you Myself: my own will shall become yours."
∽ C. S. Lewis[1]

"Whether it be something tremendously important in our eyes or the greatest triviality, nothing, nothing may be so put between ourselves and Christ that becomes a condition. For in such a case we cannot surrender ourselves to him. The surrender must be unconditional."
∽ Soren Kierkegaard[2]

"When diseased sinners come to this, that they are content to do any thing, to submit to any thing, to part with any thing, for a cure, then, and not till then, there begin to be some hopes of them. Then they will take Christ on his own terms when they are made willing to have Christ upon any terms."
∽ Matthew Henry[3]

Chapter Three:

CONVERSION

"Repent therefore and be converted, that your
sins may be blotted out, so that times of refreshing
may come from the presence of the Lord."
(Acts 3:19 NKJV)

There are many different ways of dividing humanity: racial grouping, financial status, devotion to different sports teams, and so on. However, from a spiritual standpoint, there are only two classes of people: those who have been converted to Christ and those who have not.

However, this book has been written because there is a large group of people who insist upon a third class. These are people who want the benefits of knowing God, but are unwilling to relinquish the Self-life and all the things to which it is devoted.

The sad fact is that they are only fooling themselves. They are attempting to do what the Bible clearly says is impossible. They have deceived themselves into thinking that they can live for themselves and live for God at the same time. And, of course, there is no shortage of popularity-seeking preachers who will offer them a plausible third option.

The truth is that they want their lives to revolve around *Self* with all its carnal desires. They never seem to figure out that such a life not only lies completely outside of the realm of Christianity, but it

is also certain to keep the person in a state of dissatisfaction.

William Law understood the need for conversion. He wrote, "Self is the root, the branches, the tree of all the evils of our fallen race."[4]

Those who do not submit their lives to Christ in a real way have not been *converted* to Christianity; they have been *altered* to Christianity. They have made just enough outward changes in their lives to convince themselves that they have the real thing. But being born again is not an alteration of Self; it is the obliteration of Self. To be converted means that something dramatic has occurred deep within the person. There is no such thing as a partial conversion.

All true conversions contain certain distinct elements. One person may experience all of these various steps at once, while another may be led by the Holy Spirit through a long, drawn out process which eventually brings him to make a commitment to Christ. The following list will serve as a guideline as we examine the process of conversion in greater depth.

- Conviction of Sin and Fear of God
- Spiritual Enlightenment
- Poverty of Spirit and Repentance
- Transference of Faith and Rebirth
- Sanctification and Fruit

While these various components are always in place, they may not happen in this precise order. And, as I have already stated, they can all occur at the same time. Let's take a closer look at these five steps into salvation as they are revealed in Scripture.

CONVICTION OF SIN AND FEAR OF GOD

When God begins to deal with a person, the first thing that usually takes place is that the person begins to feel a nagging sense that his life is not right with God. According to Jesus, one of the functions of the Holy Spirit would be to "convict the world concerning sin." (John 16:8) Paul later told the Thessalonian believers that "our gospel did not come to you in word only, but also in power and in the Holy Spirit and with full conviction." (I Thessalonians 1:5)

I can attest to this in my own life. I was 16-years-old when the Lord first began moving on my heart. I had been living a wretched life of crime, sex and drugs for some time. I was actually "doing time" as a juvenile when one of my old buddies told me that he had come to the Lord. I was astonished. However, before that conversation even took place, something else had been happening inside me. I tell about it in my autobiography, *Out of the Depths of Sexual Sin*:

> As those four weeks went by, an inexplicable phenomenon began to occur within me as the drug haze wore off. Although thoughts of God or Christianity never entered my mind, I started to feel a sense of guilt anytime I took the Lord's name in vain. I was living a completely degenerative life, and yet began to control my words. I had no idea that it was the conviction of the Holy Spirit…
>
> [After the conversation with my friend took place] I had a miserable evening as the thought that I could be killed and go to hell loomed over me like an ominous cloud before a thunderstorm. Honestly, I couldn't wait to go to that meeting.

My experience is not unique. Every true believer has had a similar experience. There must come a point in time when a person senses the conviction of the Holy Spirit. Without conviction there can be no repentance. It is an essential element to the process of salvation, but it is not in itself conversion.

SPIRITUAL ENLIGHTENMENT

Worldly scoffers have so ridiculed one of the most precious aspects of the Christian salvation that one never hears it uttered any longer. I am referring to the expression that someone has "seen the light."

The Bible teaches that unregenerate people live under a veil of unbelief. (II Corinthians 3:14-16) As God begins to move upon a person's heart, the person will often become aware of the spiritual domain. Suddenly, he is conscious of an entire realm that he had never before seen. John wrote, "There was the true light which, coming into the world, enlightens every man." (John 1:9) Sometimes this occurs as a natural reaction to the Holy Spirit's presence; other times it happens through the Word of God. David once wrote, "The commandment of the Lord is pure, enlightening the eyes." (Psalm 19:9) Paul later wrote, "So faith comes from hearing, and hearing by the word of Christ." (Romans 10:17)

One example of this was when Paul first visited Philippi. He found a group of women who were assembled near a river there and began sharing the gospel with them. Luke tells us that one of them whose name was Lydia "was listening; and the Lord opened her heart to respond to the things spoken by Paul." (Acts 16:14) This is an example of someone whose heart was enlightened and went on to consecrate herself to God.

However, there are others who experienced the same thing and quickly fell away. For instance, John 8 tells the story of Jesus sharing His heart with a group of Jews. Twice we are told that they "believed." (vv. 30-31) But something happened to sour them. As Jesus began talking about their need to be freed from sin, they became argumentative.

"Truly, truly, I say to you, everyone who commits sin is the slave of sin...So if the Son makes you free, you will be free indeed," Jesus told them. (vv. 34, 36) One can almost hear the pleading tone in His words. As they continued to contend with Him, He finally went right to the real problem: "Why do you not understand what I am saying? It is because you cannot hear My word. You are of your father the devil, and you want to do the desires of your father." (vv. 43-44) These people had entered the process, but as soon as they realized that it meant they had to forsake their lives, they rejected Christianity.

Variations of this exact scenario happen every day in the modern Church. There are many Christians who have been spiritually enlightened but have never taken the next step into a true conversion. As soon as someone suggests that they need to acknowledge and repent of their sin, their walls go up and their ears go deaf. They will not admit to being sinners.

When Jesus was explaining the rebirth experience to Nicodemus, He said, "...the Light has come into the world, and men loved the darkness rather than the Light, for their deeds were evil. For everyone who does evil hates the Light, and does not come to the Light for fear that his deeds will be exposed. But he who practices the truth comes to the Light..." (John 3:19-21)

Jesus was perfectly describing what has been called "The Great Refusal." In spite of what many smooth-talking preachers say today, no one enters the kingdom of God without repenting of his sin and rebellion.

POVERTY OF SPIRIT AND REPENTANCE

Having one's heart opened to the things of God is one thing; responding to that new knowledge in the right way is another. The person who experiences conviction of sin is not interested in an elaborate explanation about what is transpiring inside him. The whole process is actually very simple: either he will be humbled by what he is shown about himself or he will deny it.

The person who responds to the Holy Spirit with a sincere heart realizes that he can do nothing to escape his guilty condition. He *must* find relief from the overwhelming sense of guilt and inner turmoil. We see this process in place in the story of the Prodigal Son. When the young man had come to an end of all of his resources, he found himself in the pigpen. Jesus says, "But when he came to his senses, he said, 'How many of my father's hired men have more than enough bread, but I am dying here with hunger! I will get up and go to my father, and will say to him, 'Father, I have sinned against heaven, and in your sight; I am no longer worthy to be called your son; make me as one of your hired men.'"

This story perfectly describes a true salvation. Jesus described the spiritual enlightenment he experienced as "he came to his senses." Coinciding with this inner awakening came the sense of great remorse over the rebellion and sin of his life. His two great exclamations ("I have sinned!" and "I am not worthy!") are exactly the type of statements one would expect to hear from a person who is responding to the conviction of the Holy Spirit. *Spurious salvation experiences always lack at least one of these attitudes.*

The things this young man expressed are rarely heard today. We are not told we must deny ourselves; we are told we must love ourselves. We are not told that we are sinners who must repent; we are told that we have been emotionally traumatized and need inner healing. We are not told to consider ourselves as unworthy to be saved; we are told that we are entitled to heaven's benefits. It's no wonder that one rarely sees real conversions!

Solomon could have been writing about the current Church crowd when he wrote, "There is a class of people who are pure in their own eyes, and yet are not washed from their own filth." (Proverbs 30:12 AMP) His father understood the reason the unregenerate man won't acknowledge his sinful condition. David wrote: "…There is no fear of God before his eyes. For in his own eyes he flatters himself too much to detect or hate his sin." (Psalm 36:1-2 NIV) It is that high-minded attitude people have toward God that keeps them from repenting of their sin. Tragically, the mindset of most of today's evangelicals more closely resembles what is expressed in these two verses rather than the sincere remorse over sin that came forth from the lips of the Prodigal.

SURRENDER AND SUBMISSION

Take note of one more aspect to the Prodigal's confession. He determined that when he saw his father he would say to him, "Make me as one of your hired men." This refers to a crucial part of true repentance because it involves the will. He is saying that for the rest of his life he will do whatever he is told.

This is no small matter because it involves the person's will. It is absolutely essential that the person comes to the point of seeing that his Self directed life has been headed in the wrong direction. In short, his will must become aligned with God's will.

On a different occasion, Jesus told the following story to illustrate the necessity of repenting of self-will.

> "But what do you think? A man had two sons, and he came to the first and said, 'Son, go work today in the vineyard.' And he answered and said, 'I will, sir,' and he did not go. And he came to the second and said the same thing. But he answered and said, 'I will not,' yet he afterward regretted it and went. Which of the two did the will of his father?" They said, "The latter." Jesus said to them, "Truly I say to you that the tax-gatherers and harlots will get into the kingdom of God before you." (Matthew 21:28-31)

In this passage of Scripture, the first son conveyed the impression that he would do the will of his father: "I will, sir," he stated. Though he represented himself as one who intended to do the will of his father, he failed to follow through. The second son, on the other hand, refused from the outset. "It is my will not to do as you wish," he said. Later, having thought better of his decision, he changed his mind. Jesus said that he *regretted* his thinking. His life is offered as an example of true repentance. He had agreed to subordinate his will to that of his father's.

When considering this matter of submission, it is important to remember that it is typically reached in *stages*. Even when a person has a true conversion, it usually doesn't translate into practical submission for years to come. Something of the rule of Self is unquestionably broken. Yet, the born again experience is only the beginning aspect of this process. If the commitment to Christ is real, the day will come when there will be a greater surrender to His will. If true submission never occurs, it is proof that conversion never happened either. George Bowen paints a picture of the growing level of submission in the life of a believer:

> The soul of every believer is a kingdom where the Redeemer is seen ascending the steps of the palace so long usurped and degraded, penetrating in more or less rapid succession to its chambers, and in due time mounting, in undisputed authority, its throne. The soul is the chaos of a universe, and the work of Christ is to recreate this shattered and blasted immensity, and compel everything to circulate in harmony around the central sun.[5]

THIS GREAT SALVATION

The reason there are both real and false conversions is that not everyone who begins the process completes it. Some come under the conviction of sin but do not respond with true repentance. Others do not take their experience any further than becoming spiritually enlightened.

The Day of Pentecost provides a clear picture of a group of people who were genuinely born again. The Holy Spirit had just been poured out upon the 120 saints in the upper room. Jerusalem was filled with pilgrims there for the festival and when the believers came spilling out of the building, the commotion instantly drew a crowd of curious onlookers.

Peter, inspired by the Holy Spirit, seized the opportunity to preach a powerful message. Luke tells us that "when they heard this, they were pierced to the heart, and said to Peter and the rest of the apostles, 'Brethren, what shall we do?'" (Acts 2:37)

Peter told them to repent and be baptized as an outward sign of their new faith in Christ. Look at the type of Christianity that emerged from the conversions that took place that day:

- They were continually devoting themselves to the apostles' teaching and to fellowship,
- They were continually devoting themselves to the breaking of bread and to prayer.
- They all kept feeling a sense of awe.
- They had all things in common.
- They began selling their property and possessions and sharing them with all, as anyone might have need.
- They were continuing with one mind in the temple every day.
- They were breaking bread from house to house.
- They were taking their meals together with gladness and sincerity of heart.
- They were praising God and having favor with all the people. (Acts 2:41-47)

Now let me ask you a question: How many churches do you know that show this kind of enthusiasm for the things of God? I think we would all agree that there is little of this kind of deep passion for the Lord in America today. The standard response to this is that it is unrealistic to expect people to have this level of commitment in today's world. My question to that response is, Why?

To an unconverted person, the lifestyle described above seems too demanding, too rigid and too limited. But I want to say that this kind of Christianity is not only possible, I have witnessed it. I admit that it is rare in our current Church culture that is rife with selfishness and worldliness. Nevertheless, not only does it exist, it is the way that Christianity should be lived.

The great difference between the First Century Church and the Post-Modern Church could be summed up in the word, *life*. First Century believers didn't have elaborate programs, fancy facilities and innovative technology. But they were full of the life of God. Paul wrote, "Even when we were dead in sins, [God] hath quickened us together with Christ..." (Ephesians 2:5 KJV) Regarding this verse, W. B. Godbey wrote the following:

> "Quicken" is *suzoopoieo*, from *zoe*, life, and *poieo*, to create. Therefore, the regeneration of a sinner by the Holy Ghost is an actual *de novo* creation, as literal and unequivocal as the creation of a world out of nothing...Hence, the human spirit of a sinner is as dead as a devil in hell, till Divine life is actually created in that spirit by the Holy Spirit. Hence, the radical trouble in the Churches is not the [lack] of sanctification, but regeneration, which always reaches out for sanctification. The rosewater gospel of the popular Churches is utterly ignorant of the Bible type of regeneration, in which the Holy Ghost comes into the dead soul with the same *de*

facto creative power which flung worlds from the creative fiat into ethereal space.[6]

It is precisely this experience of having the life of God breathed into one's soul that creates a new and sustained energy for spiritual things. The following story typifies the difference between lifeless Christianity and the real thing. The young girl who wrote this testimony experienced the same lifelessness that many professing Christians live with daily. Although her story took place in the 1950's, the honest struggle she faced over how she would respond to the conviction of the Holy Spirit is so well articulated that I must include it.

> Having been born and brought up in a missionary family where spiritual values were more highly esteemed than any other thing, I kept my faith unquestioned until I went to college in America. There I was assailed by many doubts. Nothing could shake my belief in God. My parents fulfilled His conditions and were secure in His love and faithfulness, but this had nothing to do with me; I had to taste life; I had to find out for myself.
>
> After graduation my one desire was to get back to India. I liked it there. I loved the mountains, the people, the happy life I had always known. I wanted to write. I would travel, I would live!...
>
> But in India something was wrong, very wrong. Meetings, conferences, retreats, prayers—I was surrounded with them. I had to teach Sunday school, lead a young peoples' group, take devotions, give testimonies, answer those in difficulties. This I had not bargained for. I managed to struggle along for some time, knowing a bit of the technique. But what was first empty and meaningless became bitterness and filled me with contempt and rebellion...Then I realized that

everything I really wanted was out of my reach. I wanted fun; I wanted a good time in my own way. I would hear the orchestra playing dance music at the club and waves of misery swept over me. That was what I wanted, and as a missionary I was debarred. What a rigid and barren life was being imposed on me!

At Language School I met many wonderful young people whom I admired, but they all seemed so sure of their call; their religion meant something to them. I pitied them in my heart for being so simple—or was it that I envied them?

One Sunday in a desperate, almost rebellious, frame of mind I went to church, the struggle in my heart being almost unbearable. I was so unhappy something had to happen or I could not go on.

Dr. Stanley Jones was the preacher. He read his text, "Whoever will save his life shall lose it: and whosoever will lose his life for my sake shall find it" (Matt. 16:25, K.J.V.). My heart cried out, "Oh, no, not that! I do not want to lose my life. I want to live! I want happiness and beautiful things and friends. I want gaiety and popularity and a good time. I want life!" A sadness which seemed about to crush the breath out of my body engulfed me. How unfair, how cruel, how crazy—to ask me to give up life when it was the one thing I longed for—life with its music, its color, its fun!

I listened to the sermon. Step by step the way was explained; the logic was irrefutable; the paradox seemed unanswerable, so maddeningly convincing, and yet I was unwilling to accept it. It was impossible for me to give up my life whatever the promises. Then the last hymn was announced: "When I survey the wondrous cross." My eyes skimmed down over the verses. Then something like panic seized me. There was a line coming which I could not sing. Nothing could make me sing that—I would die if I had to. The second stanza began; the first line, then the second line—it was coming nearer; what should I do? How could I give up everything? It was asking too much. "O God," I cried in my heart, "what shall I do?"

Then moved by some power not of myself, I managed to sing inaudibly, "All the vain things that charm me most, I sacrifice them to His blood." It was done! Everything was gone. At that moment life seemed drained of everything. It was complete and utter emptiness. There was nothing left. But at that very moment, almost simultaneously, came an overwhelming sense of breathless joy. It seemed that I would be swept off my feet so great was the infilling, the glory. Christ Himself flooded my heart, overwhelmed me with love. In a flash it was plain—*this* was life, this abundance, this joy unspeakable and full of glory.[7]

This story perfectly paints the picture of a true conversion. This young girl was attempting to do what far too many are successfully accomplishing in our day: living the Christian life with an unconverted heart. Thank God she came to a true surrender.

However, it should be noted that not all conversions look the same. Conversion is a matter of the will, not the emotions. Many have felt the same sense of joy she experienced when they were enlightened to spiritual truths; the difference was that they did not surrender.

But how can a person know if he has experienced a genuine conversion? The Bible offers very clear instructions on how to verify the authenticity of being born again.

"Carnal doctrines do not teach you to put the flesh nature to death. They encourage you to practice sin...People have turned from God and left their first love by the millions to follow after false teachers and distorted gospels... This is the falling away today."
∽ Milton Green[1]

"The truth is that salvation apart from obedience is unknown in the sacred Scriptures...Apart from obedience, there can be no salvation, for salvation without obedience is a self-contradictory impossibility. The essence of sin is rebellion against divine authourity." ∽ A.W. Tozer[2]

"There are two extremes in religion, equally false and equally fatal. And there are two classes of hypocrites that occupy these two extremes. The first class make religion to consist altogether in the belief of certain abstract doctrines, or what they call faith, and lay little or no stress on good works. The other class make religion to consist altogether in good works, (I mean, dead works) and lay little or no stress on faith in Jesus Christ, but hope for salvation by their own deeds."
∽ Charles Finney[3]

Chapter Four

THE EVIDENCE OF FAITH

"What good is it, my brethren, if a man professes to have faith, and yet his actions do not correspond? Can such faith save him?...But, idle boaster, are you willing to be taught how it is that faith apart from obedience is worthless?" (James 2:14, 20a WNT)

For many years I thought that the greatest problem in the Church today has been a lack of discipleship. If pastors would just take the time to work with individuals—encouraging, exhorting and training them—most of the carnality, worldliness and sin amongst Christians would evaporate.

I have since changed my thinking. The best discipleship in the world cannot help an unconverted person become more godly. It would go a long way to help those who have been truly converted, but I am convinced that much of the work that goes on in the Church today is the attempt to make unbelievers *act* like believers. Vast multitudes of professing Christians have never bowed their knee to the Christ they claim to follow. If they are unconverted, the best they can hope to accomplish is to try to please God in the flesh—something that the Apostle Paul said was impossible. (Romans 8:8)

It seems that much of the problem stems from a terrible misconception over the biblical term *believe* (or the noun form, *faith*). One example I could cite comes from a message I recently saw printed in block letters across the back of a car. I offer it exactly as it was written:

DO WE WALK ON WATER ON SUNDAY
AND THEN WALK ON EVERYONE THE REST OF THE WEEK?
HE KNOWS AND LOVES US ANYWAY.

This person obviously believes that if a person claims to be a Christian, he can treat others however he wishes: God loves him no matter how he acts. This message is reminiscent of a popular bumper sticker that says: *Christians aren't perfect just forgiven.* The same inference is offered: if someone professes Christianity his actions don't matter because he enjoys the automatic forgiveness of any and all sins. Both of these messages fly directly in the face of a great number of New Testament passages that clearly state that a person's actions *do matter*; in fact, they determine his or her eternal destination.

Anyone can claim to be a follower of Christ, but "the proof is in the pudding." Does that person truly act as though he believes what the Bible says? Does his life really reflect a godly character? Does he live with the kind of utter commitment one would expect to see from a genuine believer? A person's life provides the incontrovertible evidence for whether or not he truly believes in Christ.

One of the most popular falsehoods about faith communicated today is that if a person believes that Jesus Christ lived, died and was resurrected that he is saved. Advocates of this notion quote Romans 10:9 as scriptural proof: "that if you confess with your mouth Jesus as Lord, and believe in your heart that God raised Him from the dead, you will be saved."

The key to understanding this verse lies in the phrase, *believe in your heart.* For many, belief in Christ means little more than *mentally* accepting the historical and doctrinal facts regarding Jesus Christ. This is much different than a faith born out of the heart of a person who deeply repents over a lifetime of rebellion against God's authority. Possessing "head knowledge" about spiritual information does not constitute salvation. David Kirkwood rightly asks: "What would make us think that knowing those things makes us righteous in God's eyes?"[4]

Furthermore, Scripture very clearly points out that godly behavior follows the true conversion. Paul goes on to say in the next verse: "for with the heart a person believes, resulting in righteousness…" (Romans 10:10) We see that Paul clearly taught that a righteous life would follow true faith. Kirkwood offers the following illustration to make this point:

> If you tell [a man] a deadly spider is crawling up his leg, and he smiles and continues conversing with you, you can be sure he doesn't believe you. Likewise, the person who believes in Jesus acts accordingly. His faith is evidenced by his obedience.
>
> Although many professing Christians claim to believe that Jesus is the Son of God, it's obvious by their actions that they don't believe at all. As Paul wrote, "They profess to know God, but by their deeds they deny Him…" (Titus 1:16).[5]

The same teachers who advocate a faith so weak that it doesn't bring about any real change in a person's life take their false notion one step further: they tell their adherents that they must hold onto their confession of faith no matter what! They are actually taught that this "assurance of salvation" is proof of their faith. John MacArthur writes the following:

> What lulls people into such deception? First of all, many professed Christians—and even many true Christians—hold a false doctrine of assurance. Often it is because the person who witnessed to them told

them that all they had to do was make a profession of faith, walk an aisle, raise a hand, say a prayer, and never doubt what the Lord had done in their lives. Perhaps they have been taught that to ever doubt their salvation is to doubt God's Word and integrity. Unfortunately, many evangelists, pastors, and personal workers attempt to certify a person's salvation apart from the convicting work of the Holy Spirit and the evidence of fruit with continuance in obedience to the Word (John 8:31). But we have no right to assure a person of something we cannot be certain is true.[6]

John Piper adds:

> The Bible makes it plain, I believe, that people who persistently refuse the command of Jesus' lordship have no warrant for believing that they are saved. Such people should not be comforted…In fact, Jesus seems far more eager to explode the assurance of false "professions of faith" than he is to give assurance to people who are intent on living in sin. Where does he ever bolster the "eternal security" of a person unwilling to forsake sin?[7]

Nearly every New Testament writer warned against such presumption. Paul wrote, "Test yourselves to see if you are in the faith; examine yourselves! Or do you not recognize this about yourselves, that Jesus Christ is in you—unless indeed you fail the test?" (II Corinthians 13:5) The book of Hebrews warns: "Therefore, let us fear if, while a promise remains of entering His rest, any one of you may seem to have come short of it." (Hebrews 4:1) Peter said, "Therefore, brethren, be all the more diligent to make certain about His calling and choosing you…" (II Peter 1:10) James adds, "But prove yourselves doers

of the word, and not merely hearers who delude themselves."
(James 1:22) Finally, John wrote, "The one who says, 'I have come to
know Him,' and does not keep His commandments, is a liar, and
the truth is not in him." (I John 2:4) All of these clear-cut warnings
are nonchalantly brushed aside because they don't line up with
the preconceived doctrines these people have concocted.

The truth is that these false teachers are not advocating
a faith in Christ at all; they are proposing that people should
stake their entire eternity upon a trip they once made to an altar.
They do not understand how easy it is for people to deceive
themselves.

There is an element of truth in what they propose. Scripture
does allow for the assurance of one's faith, but it is always
attached to clear evidence to support that belief. There are
certain characteristics of a person who believes in Christ. The
Bible offers these proofs of salvation as a means of allowing a
sincere person to test himself to see if he is "in the faith."*

FAITH PROVEN BY CHILDLIKENESS

*"Truly I say to you, unless you are converted and
become like children, you will not enter the kingdom
of heaven. Whoever then humbles himself as this
child, he is the greatest in the kingdom of heaven."*
(Matthew 18:3-4)

These two verses show both the evidence of a person
having been born anew and the direction of one's life after
the conversion experience. There are many things which could

---

* Scripture actually offers a number of tests one can use to determine the validity of his faith.
For instance, John gave this as one of the primary purposes for writing his first epistle: "These
things I have written to you who believe in the name of the Son of God, so that you may
know that you have eternal life." (I John 5:13) He offers seven clear-cut tests in his epistle:
walking in the light (1:5-7); regular confession of sin (1:8-10); keeping the commandments
of Jesus (2:3-4); a life that resembles Christ's life (2:6); love for the brethren (2:9-10; 3:14-19;
4:7-8); separation from the world (2:15-17; 5:4); and finally, practicing righteousness rather
than practicing sin (2:29; 3:4-10).

rightly be stated about the childlikeness of a true believer. A small child tends to be refreshingly transparent. He has not yet learned how to conceal his true nature. He is destitute of self-importance or self-ambition. He is content with the tiny world he has around him. He has also not yet developed the cold cynicism that tends to emerge as a person learns to become overly vigilant about guarding himself against deception. A small child also possesses the innocence of one who has not yet been polluted by indulging in habitual sin.

In short, it could be said that childlikeness denotes a mindset that is the diametric opposite of the lifestyle of the typical American: striving to get ahead; pushing oneself to the front position; being independent; being cynical; doing one's own will rather than really praying through to know God's will; etc.

A person cannot be taught such a mindset. It can only come about through the breaking down of the old Self-life and the emergence of the nature of Christ. As we saw in the last chapter, a conversion means that there has been a major overhauling of a person's nature.

I believe that all of the qualities of childlikeness listed above describe the kind of life the true believer is born into at salvation. But the one characteristic that describes this childlike attitude more than any other is that of trusting dependence. A young child lives completely by faith. He has not learned to trust in himself yet. Every need he has had in his young life has been provided for by his parents. He has perfect assurance of their love and faithfulness.

To be converted means to transfer one's trust from Self to God in a very real way. Indeed, the very definition of the word belief (Gk., *pisteuo*) describes this childlike trust. *Strong's Greek Dictionary* defines it: "to *have faith* (in, upon, or with respect to, a person or thing)...by implication to *entrust* (especially one's spiritual well being to Christ)."[8] (italics in original.) *Vine's Expository Dictionary* says, "to be persuaded of, and hence, to place confidence in, to trust, signifies, in this sense of the word, reliance upon, not mere credence."[9] This is precisely what Jesus meant when He said, "Whoever then humbles himself as this child, he is the greatest in the kingdom of heaven."

A spurious faith is one which expresses a certain mental confidence in the dogmas of Christianity, but true, saving faith is evidenced by a conviction within a person's heart that God can and must be trusted with all of life's decisions.

FAITH PROVEN BY CHANGE

"...lay aside the old self, which is being corrupted in accordance with the lusts of deceit...be renewed in the spirit of your mind, and put on the new self, which in the likeness of God has been created in righteousness and holiness of the truth."
(Ephesians 4:22-24)

By its very nature the Christian faith expects change. Not only is there a dramatic transformation of the person's values, perspectives, attitudes and motives at rebirth, but there is a unambiguous path laid out before him of a lifelong process of spiritual growth. Once a person receives a revelation of Calvary, he instantly understands how little he resembles Christ.

Even though he has repented of obvious sins, he recognizes the fact that much still needs to be changed in his nature. The indwelling Spirit continually convicts him of sin and helps him to sense when he has departed the narrow way of Christianity.

As time goes on, the believer matures in the faith. Sins that once held him lose their power. He becomes increasingly more Christlike. The various fruits of the Spirit become more evident in his life. His interest in the things of this world wanes as his love for God grows.

False converts, on the other hand, experience very little inward change. If they remain in the Church long enough, they will eventually take on certain Christian characteristics. This will occur just by virtue of becoming acclimated to the society of Christendom which has a somewhat nobler value system than that of the pagan world around it. They very well may hold with contempt the obvious ills of our permissive culture such as homosexuality, abortion, pornography and so on. However, that does not necessarily mean that they have experienced the inner transformation that occurs with the new birth. Such a person is still following the ways of the world and living for Self, rather than for God and His kingdom. As Kirkwood points out: He is "trusting in a grace that forgives but doesn't transform him, a grace that doesn't exist."[10]

FAITH PROVEN BY OBEDIENCE

"He who believes in the Son has eternal life; but he who does not obey the Son will not see life, but the wrath of God abides on him." (John 3:36)

Throughout the New Testament the concept of faith is clearly tied to one's obedience to God. In fact, it is impossible to have one without the other. For instance, the writer of Hebrews said that Jesus "…became to all those who obey Him the source of eternal salvation." (Hebrews 5:9)

One should never underestimate Satan's ability to work through people to introduce subtle falsehoods into the Church. During the Dark Ages, Catholicism taught a very skewed form of Christianity that was built upon religious rituals as a way to make penance for one's sins. The great need was for someone to stand forth against the prevalent misunderstanding of that day and to proclaim that one is saved by faith, not by works. God used Martin Luther to expose this falsehood for what it was.

However, on the other end of the spectrum is the notion that since faith alone saves, there is no need for works. Luther found himself forced to withstand this error as well. He wrote,

"It is impossible, indeed, to separate works from faith, just as it is impossible to separate heat and light from fire."[11] The great reformer coined a term to describe false teachers who propagated this lifeless Christianity: *antinomians.* The Greek roots of this word are *anti*, against, and *nomos*, law. In other words, these people do not want to be constrained by biblical commandments.

In our day and age, the great need is not to withstand religious ritualism or cultish legalism but a terrible antinomianism that has swept through the Church. "Unlike the legalists of Martin Luther's day, today's church-goers don't need to be told that their dead works can't save them. Rather, they need to be told that their dead faith can't save them."[12]

At a time when our culture is rife with selfishness and licentiousness, the Church should be making a strong statement about the need for holy living. While Christians do a fairly good job of denouncing outward examples of wickedness such as abortion and homosexuality, little is said about heart issues such as pride, lust and greed.

Antinomians are quick to point out that the Apostle Paul constantly stressed that a person is saved by faith and not by works of the law. Paul faced a growing threat to the newfound Church by Judaisers—Jews who had attempted to bring the Old Testament system of the law into Christianity. Like Luther, Paul was decrying the great doctrinal error of the day.

On the other hand, James witnessed people who were tending, not toward legalism but toward licentiousness. In the midst of his great chapter on the balance of faith and works, he wrote, "…faith, if it has no works, is dead, being by itself." (James 2:17) David Kirkwood explains:

> Paul and James were both speaking of being justified
> before God, and their apparent contradictory statements

are not difficult to reconcile. Paul was addressing legalists who considered the Law to be the means of salvation. Paul wanted them to know that salvation can't be earned by anyone's feeble attempt to keep the Law. Salvation is a free gift that has been provided by God's grace and is received by faith.

James, however, was addressing those who had corrupted the truth of salvation by grace through faith, reducing it to a license to sin. Their motto was "justification by faith alone," but like modern antinomians, they had redefined faith to be nothing more than a verbal profession, a faith that can be void of any corresponding acts. James wrote to refute that error...[13]

Christianity has always been evidenced by obedience. Indeed, obeying the commandments of Jesus is our means of expressing our love and gratitude to Him.

FAITH PROVEN BY FRUIT

*"...he who abides in Me and I in him, he bears
much fruit, for apart from Me you can do nothing.
If anyone does not abide in Me, he is thrown...into the
fire and they are burned." (John 15:5-6)*

Not only is a person's rebirth clear from the fact that he has transferred (or at the very least is in the process of transferring) his faith from Self to God; and that he is growing into the likeness of Christ; and that obedience to biblical commands is evident in his life; but his faith is also substantiated by the fact that other people are being spiritually affected by his life.

Some people believe that when Jesus speaks of fruit that He means the "fruit of the Spirit" as outlined in Galatians 5. Others think that the term represents the results of ministry.

Personally, I believe it is both. Unless a person is full of the Spirit of Christ, he is not going to accomplish anything of value in the kingdom of God.

It is by remaining connected in a very real way to Christ that we undergo the inner transformation that brings about Christlikeness. The aroma that comes from a godly life is what attracts others to Christ. Yes, we need the fruit of the Spirit manifested in our daily lives: *love, joy, peace, patience, kindness, goodness, faithfulness, gentleness, and self-control.* (Galatians 5:22-23) Sinners are drawn to those who exude such beautiful attributes.

Those who want to "dumb down" Christianity infer that it is acceptable for a Christian to bring little or even no fruit, but Jesus said that anyone who abides in Him will "bear much fruit." Elsewhere Jesus said that the person will bear fruit, "some a hundredfold, some sixty, and some thirty." (Matthew 13:23)

It is part of the normal Christian life to have a marked effect on the lives of other people. If a professing believer isn't clearly influencing others toward Christ, he should seriously examine whether or not he is actually in the faith.

One such example of a young believer who possesses all of these proofs of faith (trust, change, obedience and fruit) is Robert Reschar. His story is a perfect example of a person who was converted from being a pseudo-Christian into a true believer. Robert faithfully attended service at a local "Bible-believing" church. However, he was terribly addicted to food and having secret homosexual encounters. Ridden with guilt about his sexual sin, he finally confessed to his pastor. His hope was that the pastor would disciple him and truly hold him accountable for his actions. Instead, the minister offered him a position on the board of deacons.

Over the next few years his problems grew worse. By 2002, he weighed over 500 pounds and was terribly addicted to homosexuality. Nothing he heard in his church gave him any hope that he could be freed from the sin that gripped his heart and life. Finally, in total despair, he (unsuccessfully) attempted to take his own life.

Not long after this, he heard about Pure Life Ministries and entered the residential program for sexual addicts. His deep cynicism was obvious to everyone there. "I grew up in church and heard the Bible all of my life," he remembers thinking. "Why should I believe anything will be different here?"

Instead of trying to encourage Robert in his "faith," his counselor told him that he was very concerned that he had never been born again. No one had ever suggested such a thing to him. In fact, he had been taught to rest in the assurance of his salvation.

Robert took this new concern to the Lord and made a real surrender of his life to God. Something very noticeable happened within him.

One of the first signs of change was that he curbed his eating and began a regular exercise routine. Within two months he dropped 50 pounds!

He also began gaining the victory over his 15-year habit of masturbation. Little by little, he was becoming increasingly freed from the shackles of sin and fear that had bound him for many years. Each victory brought more freedom and greater hope. In fact, his last bout with masturbation occurred in early 2004. Not only has Robert found victory over sexual sin, but (as of this writing) he has also lost over 200 pounds. On top of all of that, he kicked a ten-year habit of psychotropic medication. These outward victories were wonderful, but God had a deeper work to accomplish in his life.

Six months after arriving at Pure Life, Robert graduated from the live-in program. Most men would have settled for just gaining victory over sexual sin, but Robert was not content with stopping there. He wanted to be a completely transformed man and believed God could do it. "The Lord had done something tremendous for me and I didn't want to go back to my old life. I saw the powerful work He was doing in the lives of the interns and I wanted that for myself!"

The intern program wasn't easy. He had to face the fact that there was still much in his nature that was unconquered: pride, selfishness and laziness. But Robert quietly kept battling. For nearly three years his job was to answer the phones at PLM and handle small office chores. It was far from being a glorious position and one that really tested his commitment. "There were times when I wondered if my life meant anything, but then the Lord would help me see what He was producing inside of me."

The long battle has been well worth it. He is now a ministry counselor, and his life is a shining testimony to other despairing men that they too can experience inward transformation. When he speaks in a meeting or counsels one of his men, he has something of substance to share with them. Robert's life imparts tremendous hope.

Robert's story should not be considered exceptional. God has been transforming people from the inside-out for 2,000 years. When a person is truly converted, there will be definite evidence of a living faith in Christ.

"I cannot but fear that only a comparatively
few of the visible Church are converted to God."
↪ Charles Finney[1]

"Our Lord's word 'believe' does not refer to an
intellectual act, but to a moral act. With Him 'to
believe' means 'to commit.' I have no right to say
I believe in God unless I order my life as under
His all-seeing Eye." ↪ Oswald Chambers[2]

"It will be utterly useless to plead that we
believed in Christ, unless our faith has had
some sanctifying effect and been seen in
our lives. Evidence, Evidence, Evidence will be
the one thing wanted when the books are opened
and the dead are arraigned before the bar of God.
Without some evidence that our faith in Christ
was real and genuine, we shall only rise again to be
condemned. The question will not be how
we talked and what we professed, but how we
lived and what we did. Let no man deceive
himself on this point."
↪ J.C. Ryle[3]

Chapter Five

COUNTERFEIT KINGDOM

*"The Lord said to his people, 'Stand at the
crossroads and look. Ask for the ancient paths and
where the best road is. Walk in it, and you will
live in peace.' But they said, 'No, we will not!'"*
(Jeremiah 6:16 GNB)

When Jesus began His public ministry, He immediately began talking about an unseen spiritual kingdom. "Repent," He announced, "for the kingdom of heaven is at hand." (Matthew 4:17) He then gave the remarkable Sermon on the Mount, which is a description of life in God's kingdom.

He made 91 statements about His kingdom during that unforgettable day, masterfully wrapping them all up in the single, comprehensive commandment of Matthew 7:12: "In everything, therefore, treat people the same way you want them to treat you, for this is the Law and the Prophets."

Jesus then concluded His marvelous sermon with four successive parables to reveal the difference between true and false conversion:

- The Broad Way (Matthew 7:13-14)
- False Teachers (Matthew 7:15-20)
- False Professors (Matthew 7:21-23)
- Hypocrites (Matthew 7:24-27)

CHURCH PEOPLE ON THE BROAD WAY

"Enter through the narrow gate; for wide is the gate and spacious and broad is the way that leads away to destruction, and many are those who are entering through it. But the gate is narrow (contracted by pressure) and the way is straitened and compressed that leads away to life, and few are those who find it." (Matthew 7:13-14 AMP)

In this illustration, Jesus explained that there are two roads, with two distinct groups of people marching along, heading toward destinations that are clearly opposite from each other. I have the sense that this was a sight into the unseen spiritual realm that was never far from His mind.

As obvious as it is, it should be noted that narrow does not mean broad; few does not mean many. John Bunyan, who languished in a damp, cold jail cell for years because of his refusal to quit preaching the Cross, painted a graphic picture of this spiritual reality in his classic book, *A Pilgrim's Progress*. He represents the narrow way as a difficult path where an occasional lonely straggler is seen pushing on toward his heavenly calling.

As much as seeker-sensitive pastors want to throw open the gates of heaven to anyone who ever showed the slightest inclination toward the things of God, it is clear that this parable precludes this. John MacArthur points out:

> Most people spend their lives rushing around with the crowds, doing what everyone else does and believing what everyone else believes. But as far as salvation is concerned, there is no security in numbers...
>
> The way that is broad is the easy, attractive, inclusive, indulgent, permissive, and self-oriented way of the world. There are few rules, few restrictions, and few requirements. All you need to do is profess Jesus, or

at least be religious, and you are readily accepted in that large and diverse group. Sin is tolerated, truth is moderated, and humility is ignored. God's Word is praised but not studied, and His standards are admired but not followed. This way requires no spiritual maturity, no moral character, no commitment, and no sacrifice. It is the easy way of floating downstream...[4]

It is an interesting phenomenon that the very thing that Jesus uses to illustrate the way to destruction, is what false believers use to support the notion that they are saved. They convince themselves that because everyone else around them lives like they do that surely they must be in good standing with God. They are missing the point: the Broad Way is where the masses of religious people are found.* As John Wesley said, "If many go with you, as sure as God is true, both they and you are going to hell!"[5]

One of the most honest struggles at these two gates I have ever personally witnessed was that which Jeff Cólon experienced when he was in the Pure Life Ministries live-in program. It revolved around God's call on his life to remain in Kentucky when he completed the program and to work at the ministry. Jeff had always been an obsessive controller, but the Lord was dealing with him about letting go of his own plans and making a real surrender. He shares what he experienced:

> No matter how hard I tried to avoid or evade it, God kept pressing me about this issue; in meetings, homework, counseling, and things I read in my Bible. God was tugging at my heart. I had been in the program for about five months when the Lord spoke very clearly to my inner man one day when I was out on the ridge

---

* Ray Comfort is convinced that even this first parable about the broad way is describing people who have had an experience with God—a false conversion. The point he makes is that these people also go through a gate, something that those populating the unbelieving world never do. The gate they enter is a wide gate and it leads to destruction.

praying. "You are not going back to your old life. I want you to leave all behind and serve Me."

Oh, how I wrestled that day with God! I felt like my whole insides were being torn to pieces. I knew God was speaking to me and I knew if I didn't yield to God's will, my life would be miserable and I would be in trouble.

I wanted to live this consecrated life, but I wanted to do it in New York, not Kentucky. I wanted it to fit into my own life. But the Lord made it very clear to me that day that there were two roads before me. One was narrow and had no room for my own plans or what was comfortable for me. The other was broad and had plenty of room for what I wanted to do, my life in New York, my career, my possessions and even a little place for Jesus.

I finally gave in to God and chose the narrow way. The minute I made the choice, all the pressure, anxiety, and turmoil left and a peace that surpasses all understanding came upon me. I immediately ran and called my wife. Victory, at last!

FALSE TEACHERS

"Beware of false prophets, who come to you dressed as sheep, but inside they are devouring wolves. You will fully recognize them by their fruits. Do people pick grapes from thorns, or figs from thistles? Even so, every healthy (sound) tree bears good fruit [worthy of admiration], but the sickly (decaying, worthless) tree bears bad (worthless) fruit. A good (healthy) tree cannot bear bad (worthless) fruit, nor can a bad (diseased) tree bear excellent fruit [worthy of admiration]. Every tree that does not bear good fruit is cut down and cast into the fire. Therefore, you will fully know them by their fruits." (Matthew 7:15-20 AMP)

Jesus followed the parable of the Narrow Way with another one that described deceiving ministers. The very first thing He says is to "beware of false prophets." The fact that this warning is repeated so many times regarding the last days makes this subject one of enormous importance to us today. (Matthew 24; II Thessalonians 2; II Timothy 4; II Peter 2)

There are two primary characteristics about false teachers that should be noted. First, they appear to be something they are not. Jesus exclaimed:

> "Woe to you, scribes and Pharisees, hypocrites! For you are like whitewashed tombs which on the outside appear beautiful, but inside they are full of dead men's bones and all uncleanness. Even so you too outwardly appear righteous to men, but inwardly you are full of hypocrisy and lawlessness." (Matthew 23:27-28)

These words *reveal the danger of living by outward standards without having a true change of heart.* One of the reasons people are easily deceived is that false teachers are nearly always nice people. They make others feel accepted and appreciated. They have a knack for connecting emotionally with others.

On top of that, they are orthodox in their doctrinal positions. These are not cult leaders or humanistic social reformers. They are friendly, even charismatic people, who fit in with the evangelical crowd. Jesus alluded to this on a different occasion when He said, "Woe to you when all men speak well of you, for their fathers used to treat the false prophets in the same way."

The second characteristic about false teachers is that they bring a message that appeals to the masses of people. Martyn Lloyd-Jones envisioned these charlatans standing by the narrow gate, trying to convince people that they don't have to go that way. (Luke 6:26)

Paul wrote, "For the time is coming when [*people*] will not tolerate (endure) sound and wholesome instruction, but, having ears itching [*for something pleasing and gratifying*], they will gather to themselves one teacher after another to a considerable number, chosen to satisfy their own liking and to foster the errors they hold, and will turn aside from hearing the truth and wander off into myths and man-made fictions." (II Timothy 4:3-4 AMP) Dear one, if this isn't describing what is happening today, what could he be referring to?

Peter also discussed false teachers of the end-times. Consider the following phrases from different Bible translations of II Peter 2:1-3:

- "...lying religious teachers among you," (MSG)
- "...subtly and stealthily introduce heretical doctrines," (AMP)
- "...who will cunningly introduce fatal heresies," (WEY)
- "...many will follow their sensuality," (NASB)
- "...they will have many eager disciples," (WNT)
- "...because of them the way of the truth will be maligned," (NASB)
- "...they with feigned words make merchandise of you," (KJV)
- "And in their desire for profit they will come to you with words of deceit, like traders doing business in souls," (BBE)
- "In their greed these false teachers will make a profit out of telling you made-up stories." (GNB)
- "They're only out for themselves. They'll say anything, anything, that sounds good to exploit you." (MSG)

The Lord could have been talking about modern-day America when He lamented, "An appalling and horrible thing has happened in the land: The prophets prophesy falsely, and the priests rule on their own authority; and My people love it so!" (Jeremiah 5:30-31)

FALSE PROFESSORS

"Not everyone who says to Me, 'Lord, Lord,' will enter the kingdom of heaven, but he who does the will of My Father who is in heaven will enter. Many will say to Me on that day, 'Lord, Lord, did we not prophesy in Your name, and in Your name cast out demons, and in Your name perform many miracles?' And then I will declare to them, 'I never knew you; depart from Me, you who practice lawlessness.'"
(Matthew 7:21-23)

The third parable offers a glimpse into a terrifying scene on Judgment Day where a large group of people, shivering with fear, seem to be astonished that they aren't included with God's elect. Once again we see the term *many* reminding us that there will be multitudes of professing Christians who will find themselves locked out of the kingdom of heaven on that terrible Day.

It is clear that these people consider themselves to be staunch believers. These are not those outside of the evangelical Church but within it. They have the correct doctrines. They believe what the Bible says about Christ. They go to the right churches. They are even enthusiastic about the things of God. Indeed, as each one comes forth, he frantically points out to the Judge all the spiritual things he did during his life. Tragically, there is one thing missing: a submissive, intimate relationship with Christ.

Believers are corporately called the "Bride of Christ." When Jesus told this group of people, "I never knew you," He was referring to the fact that His marriage to them had never actually been consummated. In biblical times when two people were married, the woman understood that she was joining her life to her husband's. Today in America, marriage is more of an equal combining of two lives, two careers, two sets of desires. The role of the wife in biblical times was only a step above that of the family servant. The wife forfeited her dreams and aspirations to attach herself to the husband's. She became his mate and submitted her will to his. There was a union of two wills, but it was almost a complete subjection of one to the other.

We, as the Bride of Christ, are called to abandon our own interests, plans and goals and subject them to our Lord and Husband. It is His responsibility to provide for us, protect us and bring fulfillment to our lives. When we marry Him, we align our lives with His plans and submit our wills to His. It is part of the marriage agreement, and to refuse to do it really does mean that we have never actually entered into it.

It reminds me of the story my friend and co-worker Mike Johnston has shared about his life as a homosexual before he came to Christ. When he worked in the civil service at an Air Force base, he knew other homosexual men in the Air Force who married women simply because they would receive extra benefits for having wives. They had legal marriages, but they had never given their hearts to their wives. They just wanted to use them.

This is the picture that comes to me about this group of professing Christians who are being sent to hell—the realm of the rebel. When Jesus calls them lawless, He wasn't saying that they didn't do a good enough job of keeping the rules; He was saying that they had reserved the right to run their own lives.

In our current Church culture, people think nothing of making their own plans, deciding for themselves what they want to do in life and living for themselves. But from the heavenly perspective, this lawlessness is very evil. It is not by accident that the same word used here describing these people as *lawless* (Gk. *anomos*), is also used to describe the coming Antichrist in Second Thessalonians 2. Perhaps it would interest you to know that the only commandment in the satanic bible is, "Do as thou wilt. This is the whole law."

Charles Finney uses the following illustration to bring out the seriousness of ignoring God's will in favor of one's own:

> Suppose a gentleman were to employ a clerk to take care of his store, and suppose the clerk were to continue to attend to his own business, and when asked to do what is necessary for his employer, who pays him his wages, he should reply, "I really have so much business of my own to attend to, that I have no time to do these things;" would not everybody cry out against such a servant, and say he was not serving his employer at all, his time is not his own, it is paid for, and he but served himself? [6]

Whatever a person might think about his "conversion" experience or about his religious life, the reality of it will be shown for what it truly was when he stands before God. Dr. Martyn Lloyd-Jones brings out the lesson of this parable:

> Finally, therefore, we must realize that what God wants above all else is ourselves—what Scripture calls our heart. He wants the inner man, the heart. He wants our submission. He does not want merely our profession, our zeal, our fervor, our works, or anything else. He wants us.
>
> It is possible for a man to say right things, to be very busy and active, to achieve apparently wonderful results, and yet not to give himself to the Lord. He may be doing it all for himself, and he may be resisting the Lord in the most vital place of all.
>
> And the greatest insult we can offer to God is to say: "Lord, Lord," fervently, to be busy and active, and yet to withhold true allegiance and submission from Him, to insist upon retaining control over our own lives.

We must submit to Him and His way as He has revealed it in the Bible and if what we do does not conform to this pattern, it is an assertion of our will and is disobedience. Indeed, it belongs to the type of conduct that makes Christ say to certain people: "Depart from me, ye that work iniquity." He calls them "workers of iniquity" because, in the last analysis, they were doing it to please themselves and not in order to please Him. Let us then solemnly examine ourselves in the light of these things.[7]

HYPOCRITES

"Therefore everyone who hears these words of Mine and acts on them, may be compared to a wise man who built his house on the rock. And the rain fell, and the floods came, and the winds blew and slammed against that house; and yet it did not fall, for it had been founded on the rock. Everyone who hears these words of Mine and does not act on them, will be like a foolish man who built his house on the sand. The rain fell, and the floods came, and the winds blew and slammed against that house; and it fell, and great was its fall."
(Matthew 7:24-27)

In the final parable, Jesus painted a picture of two different men who heard His words. Each has built a house for himself, representing his spiritual life which becomes his eternal abode. On the surface, both houses appear to be identical. The fact that they were both lashed by the same storm seems to indicate that the men lived near each other. They probably attended the same church, heard the same teachings and sang the same hymns.

The difference is found beneath the surface. The foundation of their lives is said to revolve around whether or not they actually lived the words of Jesus. The man who obeyed Scripture in his daily life is said to be wise. The man who heard the preaching and read the Word but did not actually live it out is called foolish.

In biblical terminology, a fool is someone who does not think through the consequences of his actions. He lives in the "now." Every action he takes in life is done through the unseen motive of what he is going to get out of it for himself in the temporal. Yes, he has made a profession of Christ with the idea of going to heaven, but the multitude of decisions and choices he makes in his everyday life reveals the true condition of his heart. A fool isn't honest with himself. He likes to think of himself as a godly person headed for eternal life, but the reality is that he is living for himself. Thoughts of God and eternal things do not dominate his thinking as he goes through each day. James wrote of those who are "merely hearers who delude themselves." (James 1:22)

By contrast, the wise person is continually aware of how his thoughts, words and actions appear in the light of Scripture. The indwelling Spirit of God directs his actions, convicts him of sin, chastises him when he gets off track and leads him in the will of God.

One can get a hint of what is actually happening inside these two men by the way they respond to biblical commandments. There are probably two thousand commandments in the New Testament alone, but just as an example, consider what Jesus said in the preceding chapter: "Do not store up for yourselves treasures on earth…" (Matthew 6:19) John Wesley once pointed out the fact that this is a commandment every bit as real as, "Do not commit adultery."

A sincere believer reads that verse and immediately takes an inventory of his life. "Am I really obeying this command? Or is my life one of accumulating possessions and living in a lust for what this world offers? How can I better help others in need?" Such questions come to the mind of the true believer because the Holy Spirit resides within him. It is the constriction of the narrow way.

The false professor has a very wide boundary around his

life. He obeys those commandments that are outward in nature and don't really impede the lifestyle he has chosen for himself. Just like the wise man, he doesn't cuss, commit adultery, drink alcohol or smoke tobacco. He too goes to church and lives the outward Christian life. All of this will remain intact until the storms of God's dealings come to visit him. Then the truth will come forth that he has never really been converted. Self remains immovable on the throne of his heart. Ray Comfort stresses that these people have had some spiritual experience:

> When the Scriptures say he that "hears" these sayings and doesn't do them, it uses the same word it uses for the wise man—*akouo*, which means "to understand." So Scripture is not speaking about those who are in ignorance, but of those who *understand* the sayings of Jesus…The door of salvation hinges upon obedience. A genuine convert will bring forth fruit to confirm his salvation— "Even so, *every* good tree bears good fruit…" "Fruit" is evidence of the work of the Holy Spirit in the life of the believer. [8]

There is one more matter that must be mentioned. Each of these parables gravely touches upon the final end for the people involved. Those on the Broad Way go to their "destruction." (v. 12) The false teachers are "cut down and thrown into the fire." (v. 19) The false professors are separated from Christ forever. (v. 23) The eternal dwelling constructed by the foolish man fell — "and great was its fall." (v. 27)

The Sermon on the Mount depicts the normal Christian life. The demands it makes upon the believer's life are impossible to obey *unless the Spirit of the Living God is actually dwelling within the person.* I believe the reason that so few actually live this kind of Christianity is owing to the fact that most professing evangelicals have never really been converted and are therefore not indwelt by the Holy Spirit.

Jesus plainly tells us that it is a narrow path. There are many who are determined to create a road of their own making. Every day of their lives is spent furthering it in their own direction. But the "ancient path" is fixed precisely where God has ordained it to be. It will not be shifted around by the whims of man. If not one single human being ever traverses it again, it remains where God has established it.

Hanging a sign on the Broad Way which reads, "Narrow Path," does not make it so. It is sheer delusion and folly to think that just because everyone else is on the Broad Way that somehow it is acceptable to God. Its popularity should suggest the very opposite.

Jesus clearly stated His case about the way that leads to life and the way that leads to destruction. It is our responsibility to take His warnings seriously. Indeed, it is urgent that each of us take a sober inventory of our lives according to Scripture. If the door of salvation hinges upon obedience to Christ, one should earnestly ask, Will it swing open for me?

Perhaps the challenging words of John Wesley regarding the narrow way would serve as an apt conclusion to this chapter:

> How thinly are they scattered over the earth, whose souls are enlarged in love to all mankind; and who love God with all their strength, who have given him their hearts, and desire nothing else in earth or heaven! How few are those lovers of God and man, that spend their whole strength in doing good unto all men; and are ready to suffer all things, yea, death itself, to save one soul from eternal death!...
>
> Now, then, "strive to enter in at the strait gate," being penetrated with the deepest sense of the inexpressible danger your soul is in, so long as you are in a broad way...[9]

"The ungodly on earth ignorantly dance for joy when they hear pastors speak about the love and mercy of God, but they will be the beneficiaries of neither, unless they repent."
~ William C. Nichols[1]

"Is hell so sweet, is everlasting torment so much to be desired, that therefore ye can let go the glories of heaven, the bliss of eternity?...Better a brief warfare and eternal rest, than false peace and everlasting torment." ~ Charles Spurgeon[2]

"What folly can be greater than to labor for the meat that perisheth, and neglect the food of eternal life?" ~ John Bunyan (on his death bed)[3]

"How shall I feel at the judgment, if multitudes of missed opportunities pass before me in full review, and all my excuses prove to be disguises of my cowardice and pride? "
~ Dr. W.E. Sangster[4]

Chapter Six:

TWO JUDGMENTS

*"But because you are stubborn and refuse to turn
from your sin, you are storing up terrible punishment
for yourself...He will pour out his anger and wrath on
those who live for themselves..." (Romans 2:5-8 NLT)*

O ne of the chief characteristics of pseudo-Christians
is that they have lied to themselves about their
relationship to God. They have been unwilling to
submit to God's authority, to obey His Word and to live the
Christian life as it is outlined in Scripture. They have been
very dishonest with themselves about the motivations of
their actions. They have continually viewed themselves in
the most favorable light, granting themselves the benefit of
any doubt. They have conveyed this exaggerated image of
their spirituality to those around them. The Bible calls them
hypocrites.

However, when this life has concluded and they stand before
the Almighty, every motive (I Corinthians 4:5), attitude toward
others (Matthew 7:2), word (Matthew 12:36-37), deed (Romans 2:6-8)
and even secrets of their hearts (Romans 2:16) will be exposed *in
truth* for what they truly were. The reality of what they really
believed and lived will be unraveled and laid bare to the searching
gaze of Him who gave His life for sincere believers.

Jesus Christ continually kept the subject of eternity before His hearers. Over and over He talked about the judgment every human would face. And the most fearful statements about the torments of hell came from His loving lips.

In nearly every parable, Jesus provided a glimpse into the process of judgment. The basic meaning of the word *judge* (Gk. *krino*) is to separate; from there it naturally progresses to the idea of separating good from evil and true from false. The point of the parables is to help the reader see important differences between the people groups being represented.

The picture presented in the "Broad Way" (Matthew 7:13-14) is that the mass majority of people are headed for destruction; only the few who stand out as oddballs will enter heaven.

The parable of the "False Prophets" (Matthew 7:15-20) reveals that the reality of the inner lives of Christian teachers will be thoroughly examined during the Judgment.

The parable of the "False Professors" (Matthew 7:21-23) is a picture of what will happen to those who were deeply involved in Christian work and yet would not submit to God's will. They were, in the final analysis, rebels at heart.

The parable of the "Two Houses" (Matthew 7:24-27) reveals that, although some have all the outward trappings of Christianity, Judgment will reveal that in their hearts they never really obeyed Christ. Those who pick and choose which commandments they will obey fall into this category.

In the story of the "Sower and the Seed" (Matthew 13:3-23), Jesus offers four different types of Christians. The veracity of the person's faith is proven by the fruit he has brought forth.

The parables of the "Wheat and Tares" (Matthew 13:24-30, 37-43) and the "Dragnet" (Matthew 13:47-50) both establish the fact that there are true and false believers alongside each other in this world.

The parable of the "Fig Tree" (Luke 13:6-9) reveals the fact that Jesus expects to see fruit in a Christian's life. If He continues to find a fruitless tree, the time will come that it will be cut down.

Jesus' discourse on the Last Days offers four parables especially aimed at the professing Christians alive prior to His Second Coming. The "Evil Slave" (Matthew 24:45-51) shows a complete disregard for those in his charge and has given himself over to the pleasures of earthly life.

The "Foolish Virgins" (Matthew 25:1-13) were shut out of the kingdom because of their flippant attitude toward the return of Christ. They did not take it seriously enough to prepare themselves.

The "wicked, lazy slave" in the parable of the "Talents" (Matthew 25:14-30) is doomed because of his unwillingness to invest his life and resources in the kingdom of God.

The "goats" in the parable of the "Sheep and Goats" (Matthew 25:31-46) are likewise expelled from heaven for their unwillingness to extend mercy to people in need. James later wrote, "For judgment will be merciless to one who has shown no mercy; mercy triumphs over judgment." (James 2:13)

As we saw earlier, every person alive is moving toward that day when his life will be scrutinized: "…it is appointed for men to die once and after this comes judgment." (Hebrews 9:27) Jesus, who has been given the responsibility to judge mankind (John 5:22), spoke of the certainty of this Day. "…an hour is coming, in which all who are in the tombs will hear His voice, and will come forth; those who did the good deeds to a resurrection of life, those who committed the evil deeds to a resurrection of judgment." (John 5:28-29)[*]

We see here that all mankind will be separated into two great assemblies. Charles Finney commented on the clear distinction in these two groups of people.

---

[*] In a sermon on II Corinthians 5:10, John Piper describes the Judgment as a court scene whereby a person's works are brought forth as evidence to reveal whether their faith in Christ was alive or dead.

The Bible divides all the human race into two classes only; the righteous and the wicked. Those are righteous who have true faith in Christ, whose spirit is consecrated to God, who live a heavenly life on earth, and who have been renewed by the Holy Ghost. Their original selfishness is subdued and slain, and they live a new life through the ever present grace of Christ Jesus.

Right over against them in character are the wicked, who have not been renewed in heart—who live in selfishness…self is the great and only ultimate end of their life; these are in the scriptural sense, the wicked.[5]

Although the Bible provides glimpses about the various aspects of judgment, ultimately there are only two. The "Great White Throne Judgment" is the final separation of the lost from God. Those who have been found written in the "book of life" will stand before Christ at the Bema Seat Judgment to determine what, if any, rewards they shall receive in the hereafter.

THE GREAT WHITE THRONE JUDGMENT

"Then I saw a great white throne and Him who sat upon it, from whose presence earth and heaven fled away, and no place was found for them. And I saw the dead, the great and the small, standing before the throne, and books were opened; and another book was opened, which is the book of life; and the dead were judged from the things which were written in the books, according to their deeds…And if anyone's name was not found written in the book of life, he was thrown into the lake of fire." (Revelation 20:11-15)

There are a number of interesting clues provided in this glimpse of judgment that are worth noting. First, we see the terrifying presence of Jehovah sitting on His throne. So overwhelming is His holiness and omnipotence that even heaven and earth want to flee. Standing in front of that throne is a vast throng of shivering, cowering, naked wretches who cannot hide from His penetrating gaze. Although they would give anything to escape—anything!—there is simply nowhere to run.

Each person is brought forward one at a time in front of that astonished multitude. A book of remembrance is opened which contains everything that represented their lives while on earth. Not one single deed or thought is overlooked. The true character of the person is exposed before all. One by one, each person is judged and then thrown into the vast underworld of fire and torment, represented here as a lake of fire.

One of the clearest descriptions I have ever read of what a lost person will experience during judgment was given by a medical doctor named George Ritchie. He was a young soldier preparing to be shipped overseas during World War II when he developed a case of tuberculosis. It quickly escalated and he died for several minutes before being resuscitated. During that brief time he was shown certain aspects of eternity. At one point he was brought before the Lord to be judged. As Dr. Ritchie described it, in some inexplicable way, everything he had ever thought or done was played out before him.

Every detail of twenty years of living was there to be looked at. The good, the bad, the high points, the run-of-the-mill. And with this all-inclusive view came a question. It was implicit in every scene and, like the scenes themselves, seemed to proceed from the living Light beside me…

What did you do with your life?

It seemed to be a question about values, not facts: what did you accomplish with the precious time you were allotted? And with this question shining through them, these ordinary events of a fairly typical boyhood seemed not merely unexciting but trivial. Hadn't I done anything lasting, anything important? Desperately

I looked around me for something that would seem worthwhile in the light of this blazing Reality.

It wasn't that there were spectacular sins, just the sexual hang-ups and secretiveness of most teenagers. But if there were no horrendous depths, there were no heights either. Only an endless, shortsighted clamorous concern for myself. Hadn't I ever gone beyond my own immediate interests, done anything other people would recognize as valuable? At last I located it, the proudest moment of my life:

"I became an Eagle Scout!"

Again, words seemed to emanate from the Presence beside me:

That glorified you.

It was true.[6]

This is the judgment the false Christian will face. The unavoidable fact will emerge that his life completely revolved around himself. He may possess a great deal of information about God's kingdom, but that knowledge will now serve as his accuser. Being exposed to spiritual truth only increases responsibility to live it out in a very real way.

One might suppose that the nominal Christian who forced himself to go to church every week and obeyed some of the commandments of Scripture would receive a lighter punishment than those who never bothered with church; actually Jesus claimed that the opposite is true. He addressed this subject on two different occasions.[†]

"And that slave who knew his master's will and did not get ready or act in accord with his will, will receive many lashes, but the one who did not know it, and

---

† Actually, in addition to the two explicit passages I quote here, this truth is also touched upon in Matthew 23:14, Luke 11:31-32 and James 3:1.

committed deeds worthy of a flogging, will receive but
few. From everyone who has been given much, much
will be required; and to whom they entrusted much, of
him they will ask all the more." (Luke 12:47-48)

"And you, Capernaum, will not be exalted
to heaven, will you? You will descend to Hades;
for if the miracles had occurred in Sodom which
occurred in you, it would have remained to this day."
(Matthew 11:23-24)

In both cases, we find people who had considered their
position to be something it was not. The slave is given many
lashes (whatever horrifying reality that represents!) because
he knew his master's will but did not do it. The people of
Capernaum had heard the sermons and seen the miracles of
Jesus but did not obey Him. Their familiarity with spiritual things
only hardened their hearts.

So it is with hypocrites of all ages. Like Judas, they have
emerged from a place of intimacy with Christ only to deny Him.
They have felt His love, enjoyed hearing sermons about Him,
obeyed some of His commandments and even held a certain
degree of affection for Him. Yet, in spite of being allowed to
be in such a privileged place, their testimony to the world about
Him is that He is an imposter.

"Listen," their lives say, "I've been with Jesus. I've seen
Him work in my life. I've received a multitude of His graces
and blessings. I've been in awesome worship services where
you could feel His presence. Yes, I have tried Him, but do
you know what? I have found Him wanting. Christ promised
me joy unspeakable, but I have found only drudgery. He
promised me peace beyond comprehension, but I am still
plagued by stress and uncertainty. He promised me living
waters, but I have found only the stale waters of broken

cisterns. I will continue to follow Him but only at a distance. I will retain my old worldly loves because I have found that they alone satisfy."

"They profess to know God," Paul writes, "but by their deeds they deny Him…" (Titus 1:16) Peter adds that "…because of them the way of the truth will be maligned." (II Peter 2:2)

Adam Clarke wrote that judgment "will rank semi-infidel Christians in the highest list of transgressors, and purchase them the hottest place in hell! Great God! save the reader from this destruction!"[7]

Woe unto people who have spent their lives in church but by their lives have denied Christ! Who can comprehend the utter horror they will face when their treachery is revealed to all? What human words could be expressed to properly describe the hell that awaits Apostate Christians?

THE BEMA SEAT JUDGMENT

"Therefore we also have as our ambition, whether at home or absent, to be pleasing to Him. For we must all appear before the judgment seat (Gk. bema) of Christ, so that each one may be recompensed for his deeds in the body, according to what he has done, whether good or bad. Therefore, knowing the fear of the Lord, we persuade men…" (II Corinthians 5:9-11)

Those who have been found in the "book of life" will be redirected to a different judgment: the *Bema Seat Judgment*. Even here we can see that there will be a separating of good and evil. The life of each believer will be thoroughly examined. Sin which has been repented of will be the only aspect of the person's life which will not be exposed. True believers will not face the issue about whether or not they will go to heaven; this judgment is to determine the eternal value of their lives. The overriding question they will face is whether or not and to what degree they exhibited the love of God to other people. Paul offers a fascinating glimpse into this special judgment for believers.‡

> For no man can lay a foundation other than the one
> which is laid, which is Jesus Christ. Now if any man
> builds on the foundation with gold, silver, precious
> stones, wood, hay, straw, each man's work will become
> evident; for the day will show it because it is to be
> revealed with fire, and the fire itself will test the quality
> of each man's work.
>
> If any man's work which he has built on it remains,
> he will receive a reward. If any man's work is burned up,
> he will suffer loss; but he himself will be saved, yet so
> as through fire. Do you not know that you are a temple
> of God and that the Spirit of God dwells in you? If
> any man destroys the temple of God, God will destroy
> him, for the temple of God is holy, and that is what you
> are. (I Corinthians 3:11-17)

At first glance it seems as though Paul is painting a picture
of two distinct Christians: one whose life is made up of
the imperishable riches of godliness and the other whose
life is shown to be as worthless as a cardboard shack. His
comments seem to refute what Jesus had said earlier about
those who knew Him but did not obey Him. Adding to the
confusion is the fact that earlier in the same chapter Paul
told the Corinthians that they were "infants in Christ" and
"fleshly."

Be that as it may, there are a few things that stand out in this
chapter that will bring clarity to the subject. First of all, while it
is clear that the Corinthians were immature in their faith, Paul
did tell them that they were "in Christ." Actually, historical

---

‡ While the context of Paul's metaphor is actually referring to the quality of ministers'
teaching, the point he makes remains true and offers valuable insights into the judgment a
believer faces regarding his spiritual life.

facts help to clear up the confusion. It had been only five years since Paul had first visited Corinth when he wrote these words to them. Every one of them was a spiritual babe. Not only that, it should also be noted that they had not been raised in a Christianized nation but in a very wicked, pagan culture. Perhaps he had hoped for better from them by this point, but the fact remains that they were still fairly new to the faith.

We can also learn some valuable insights from his metaphor about the two houses. At once we are reminded of the parable in the Sermon on the Mount where Jesus employed the same imagery. (Matthew 7:24-27) Unlike the man's structure which had been built upon the unstable soil of disobedience, these houses are both said to be founded upon Jesus Christ. The man who built his foundation on the sand never had a sincere intention to obey the words of Jesus. If he could fit the expectations of Christianity into his life, well and good. But when it came right down to it, he was his own master. The people Paul is describing had clearly been born again. Whatever may be said about the two structures he described, they both had the right foundation.

It should also be noted that he is not describing people; he is talking about Christian work. Jesus used contrasting people in most of His parables to show the difference between true and false believers. Paul, on the other hand, was making the point that the motivation of the believer's spiritual work will be examined when he stands before the Lord.

As far as I can tell, *every* sincere believer has done things in the name of Christ that will not stand up under the fire of judgment. I can certainly look back at things I have done and see that some were clearly motivated by Self. We are all self-centered by nature and only the work we have done in the Spirit will prove to have been effective and eternal. Jesus made this clear when He said, "I am the vine, you are the branches; he who abides in Me and I in him, he bears much fruit, for apart from Me you can do nothing." (John 15:5) The truth is that most of our work for

God contains a mixture of Self and godliness in it. Judgment will precisely differentiate the person's motives.

Paul did not infer that there will be some people who stand before Christ with nothing but "gold, silver, and precious stones," while others have nothing to show for their lives but "wood, hay and straw." This is not meant to be an "either-or" metaphor. Scripture is very clear that those who have nothing to show for their lives are not saved. As we have seen, Jesus said, "Every tree that does not bear good fruit is cut down and thrown into the fire." (Matthew 7:19) James wrote, "…faith without works is dead." (James 2:26)

The people being described in Paul's metaphor will all reach the heavenly shores. True, some "will be saved, yet so as through fire." In the same way Paul himself would arrive on the shores of Malta on a scrap of wood, they will arrive with little to show for their lives. Others will glide into the celestial harbor laden with a cargo of "gold, silver, and precious stones." As Peter said, "Thus there will be richly and abundantly provided for you entry into the eternal kingdom of our Lord and Savior Jesus Christ." (II Peter 1:11 AMP)

The truth is that only God knows the difference between those who are saved "as through fire" and those who are essentially unconverted.

TWO SCENES FROM BEMA

If every saint will one day enjoy the same blanket pardon of sin, trod the same streets of gold and worship before the same Throne, why should any of us be concerned about spiritual growth? If all the benefits of heaven await every believer, why should we fight for a holier life, pursue a deeper consecration to God, or desire to be conformed into His image? Why not just live for ourselves and enjoy the pleasures and amusements of this world while we have them?

Many people have a very carnal and earthly perspective about heaven. To them, it is a place where there is a lot of gold and people are happy. Those things may be true, but it is certainly a very immature and superficial idea about what eternity holds for the believer. Scripture plainly teaches that there will be a hierarchy in heaven established by immutable spiritual laws. Consider some of the things Jesus said about this subject.

- "Whoever then annuls one of the least of these commandments, and teaches others to do the same, shall be called least in the kingdom of heaven; but whoever keeps and teaches them, he shall be called great in the kingdom of heaven." (Matthew 5:19)
- "Whoever exalts himself shall be humbled; and whoever humbles himself shall be exalted." (Matthew 23:12)
- "His master said to him, 'Well done, good and faithful slave. You were faithful with a few things, I will put you in charge of many things; enter into the joy of your master.'" (Matthew 25:23)
- "Blessed are you when men hate you, and ostracize you, and insult you, and scorn your name as evil, for the sake of the Son of Man. Be glad in that day and leap for joy, for behold, your reward is great in heaven. For in the same way their fathers used to treat the prophets." (Luke 6:22-23)

One can see how the way we lived our lives will have a direct effect on what we receive in heaven. However, I want to bring it down to earth and make it a little more clear. Consider the following scenarios.

Word spread quickly that Karen Smith had just crossed the River Glorious. As the Lord looked on approvingly, she was mobbed by those whose lives she had affected during her lifetime. First to meet her was Amber, a neighbor girl who had been addicted to drugs. Time and again Karen had shown kindness to her, and after overdosing one night and wanting to find answers for her life she went to her compassionate neighbor. Karen led her to Christ and spent months discipling her in the faith.

Then there was her brother Will. He had been a successful stockbroker while on earth and never saw his need for Christ. Although Karen spent years earnestly praying for him, nothing seemed to change. Then, all of the sudden, he began to see the emptiness of his life and a co-worker led him to the Lord. When he arrived in heaven and saw his life played out before him, he saw how his sister's persistent intercession had made it possible for the Holy Spirit to work in his heart.

There were also a number of patients from the local convalescent hospital. For years Karen spent her Saturday mornings there. She would simply go from room to room, visiting lonely people, showing an interest and sharing her faith with them when she felt there was an opening. A number of them were so affected by her life that they came to a saving knowledge of Jesus Christ.

During the 23 years she was a believer, many people had been touched by Karen's life. The line of people stretched into the distance—each one grateful because this woman had valued them individually, in one way or another laying down her life for them.

Over and over again, one could hear Karen protesting against their displays of affection. "You give me too much credit; it was the Lord alone who saved you."

"Yes," would come the reply, "but you were the one person concerned enough to pray for me, to take time to help me, to tell me the truth." Then came the inevitable shower of hugs and kisses.

Eventually, having escaped this outpouring of love, Karen was brought before the Lord. What she did for each soul was shown before a vast multitude of angelic beings and redeemed souls. "There is joy in the presence of the angels of God over one sinner who repents." (Luke 15:10) That joy and gratitude was now directed toward her as if she were a soldier returning home to a hero's welcome. In some inexplicable way, every soul she had cared for on earth was now a jewel in a crown she would enjoy forevermore.

Like Karen, Pastor Ben also found himself standing before the Lord. He was elated when an angel informed him that his spiritual biography would be played out before the host of heaven—heroes from the Old Testament, the apostles, great missionaries, martyrs and saints from all ages. It was clear all were anxious to see what victories he had won for Christ.

As the scenes of his life played out before that great cloud of witnesses, a horrifying and inescapable reality emerged: nearly his entire 30 years of ministry had been for Self. In that moment, he saw a lifetime of service in the kingdom of God that had produced little fruit, little real results, and little by way of eternal rewards.

What stood out was that he had been far more concerned about building a successful ministry—one that gained him prestige and worldly honor—than he had been about the precious souls who had been entrusted into his care.

The worst aspect of Ben's experience was seeing the deep disappointment spread across every face—especially that Face that had been spit upon and beaten for the sake of others.

At that moment, a flash of fire burst forth from the Throne and burned up nearly all his work. There was little left to show for a lifetime of Christian service.

How about you, dear one? Which judgment is awaiting you? Are you absolutely certain that you see evidence of salvation in your life?

If you are truly a believer in Christ, what will be shown when your life is played out for all your fellow heaven-dwellers to see? Will you arrive in heaven with a rich cargo of heavenly treasures or will you "be saved, yet so as through fire?" You still have time to "Store up for yourselves treasures in heaven." (Matthew 6:20)

If you are not a true believer, the judgment which awaits you is more horrible than my words can convey. As disturbing and unappealing as the subject may be, we must examine what awaits those who have never truly been converted.

"So apostates come at last to nothing, and therefore must look for nothing better than to be cast off for ever." ❧ John Trapp[1]

"The majority of the church does not care about a perishing world and a hell that enlarges itself every moment...If only the church could gaze into the depths of hell for just a minute, to hear the cries of the damned, to smell the flesh that is ever burning but never consumed; to feel the unending despair of utter hopelessness, to hear the hatred for God that spews forth from the lips of the justly condemned. It would change us, utterly and absolutely change us." ❧ Glenn Meldrum[2]

"Look! Look! Look with solemn eye through the shades that part us from the world of spirits, and see that house of misery which men call hell! Ye cannot endure the spectacle...and when ten thousand times ten thousand years shall have rolled away, they will no more have made satisfaction to God for their guilt than they have done up till now." ❧ Charles Spurgeon[3]

Chapter Seven:

THE PLACE OF HYPOCRITES

*"Therefore hell hath enlarged herself, and opened
her mouth without measure: and their glory, and
their multitude, and their pomp, and he that
rejoiceth, shall descend into it." (Isaiah 5:14 KJV)*

Flalse converts have their "own place" (Acts 1:25), but it will not be in the Land of Glory. Instead, they will be cut "in pieces and assign[ed] a place with the hypocrites; in that place there will be weeping and gnashing of teeth." (Matthew 24:51) Jesus said of Judas, "It would have been good for that man if he had not been born." (Mark 14:21) He had built his own eternal house of punishment, and the same can be said of false Christians.

Our age has produced a deep cynicism that has made hell seem as though it is the folly of someone's imagination. It is interesting that no one argues the existence of heaven. It is only the existence of hell which is questioned. Yet, whether or not today's cultural Christianity embraces the doctrine of hell does not alter the reality of it. Scripture is very clear that hell is a real place and we must come to grips with the fact that every day people are plunging into it. It is talked about so often that a person would have to do violence to Scripture to believe otherwise.

Although it is no longer considered politically correct to preach or teach about sinners being sent to hell, people must be warned about it. One of the terrible consequences to this lack of teaching in the Body of Christ has been that worldly and unbiblical perspectives about eternal punishment have arisen. I will briefly convey three of the more common false notions and do my best to refute them.

NUMBER ONE:
GOD WOULD NOT SEND A GOOD PERSON TO HELL.

This is one of the common myths that has emerged from the ranks of unbelievers. The underlying supposition is that most people are "good" and that hell is reserved for sinners, such as Adolph Hitler, who were decidedly and plainly evil natured. This nonsense is even embraced by many sentimental Christians who imagine that nearly everyone goes to heaven because God is merciful.

First of all, Scripture clearly rebuffs this notion. Paul wrote, "There is none righteous, no not one." (Romans 3:10) Man's idea of what is good is terribly distorted. It is tantamount to an insane person in an asylum comparing himself to those around him and declaring himself to be in his right mind! In the sight of a holy God, who could possibly consider himself as being good or as deserving of heaven?

Many churchgoers possess human goodness, but make no mistake about it: at the root of it is Self-love. They are morally good because they believe that they will derive some benefit from it for themselves. The truth is that there are those who would be morally good even if they didn't believe there was a God. Just because a person once said the "sinners' prayer," goes to church and avoids obvious sin does not mean that he has truly been converted.

Part of the misconception here comes from a faulty

understanding of the nature of sin. When most people think of sin, the first things that come to their minds are obvious sins like murder, theft, fornication, etc. The real issue of sin has more to do with submission or rebellion to God's authority. That is why there are millions of "good people" in hell. Yes, they lived upright lives and even went to church. But down in the depths of their hearts, they were their own master and refused to bend their knee to the Savior. They were not sent to hell because of flagrant sin but because they refused to renounce what they considered as being their right to self-determination.

NUMBER TWO:
THE IDEA OF ETERNAL DAMNATION DOES NOT RECONCILE WITH WHAT THE BIBLE CLAIMS ABOUT GOD'S LOVE.

The Bible expresses the exact truth about God's nature when it claims, "...God is love." (I John 4:8) The Bible also teaches that He does not take pleasure in the death of the wicked. (Ezekiel 33:11) "The Lord...is patient toward you, not wishing for any to perish but for all to come to repentance." (II Peter 3:9) That's why He sent His Son to die on the Cross.

However, life on earth is probationary in nature. The purpose of our time here is that we might decide once and for all if we want to be a part of (and subject to the laws of) God's kingdom or if we would prefer to remain detached from that realm and live for ourselves. God has given us His Word to show us the way into salvation. He has sent His Son to die on the Cross so that we might have that salvation. If people show by their neglect or outright rejection that they do not care to be a part of His kingdom, that does not make Him unmerciful.

One aspect of judgment can be illustrated from our own court system. For a period of time, I served as a bailiff in the Criminal Courts Building in Los Angeles. There were times a defendant appeared to whom, for whatever reason, the judge clearly wanted to extend mercy. However, under pressure from the taxpayers, the California legislature had enacted mandatory sentencing guidelines. Even if a judge wanted to release a criminal, the guidelines forced a particular sentence.

In the same manner, the justice system which comes forth from God's holy character requires that unrepentant sinners be sentenced to hell, no matter how much love He feels for them. On numerous occasions the Lord taught that He has done everything possible to bring His hearers into His kingdom. (Isaiah 5:1-7; Matthew 11:16-24; Luke 13:6-9) Their refusal was not because of a lack of effort on His part.

Even though love longs to show kindness, perfect holiness demands justice. Hell is a place for those who have shown they do not want to live in the kingdom of God. As C.S. Lewis said, "I willingly believe that the damned are, in one sense, successful rebels to the end; that the doors of hell are locked on the inside."[4]

But even beyond that, what kind of judge would we deem God to be if He allowed law-breakers to go free? What would we think of a Superior Court judge who, in the name of mercy, refused to hold criminals accountable for their actions? Our citizens wouldn't stand for it! Yet how hypocritical it is for people to expect God to let people go unpunished who have continually flouted and shown disdain for the rules of His kingdom.

NUMBER THREE:
ETERNAL TORMENT IS A PUNISHMENT THAT
DOES NOT FIT THE CRIME.

One can only marvel at the utter lack of logic in this reasoning. If a person has come into some comprehension of the horrible nature of hell, what would stop him from doing everything in his power to avoid it? Jonathan Edwards uses piercing and irrefutable logic to expose the underlying insincerity of this thinking.

As great as [eternal punishment] is, you have made
nothing of it. When God threatened to inflict it on
you, you did not mind his threatenings, but were bold
to disobey him, and to do those very things for which
he threatened this punishment...

If you should forbid a servant to do a given thing,
and threaten that if he did it you would inflict some
very dreadful punishment upon him...and you should
continue to repeat your commands and warnings, still
setting out the dreadfulness of the punishment, and
he should still, without any regard to you, go on again
and again to disobey you to your face...could you take
it any otherwise than as daring you to do your worst?
But thus have you done towards God; you have had his
commands repeated, and his threatenings set before
you hundreds of times, and have been most solemnly
warned; yet have you notwithstanding gone on in
ways which you knew were sinful, and have done the
very things which he has forbidden, directly before
his face.[5]

GLIMPSES OF HELL

The Bible does not offer extensive teaching on exactly
what hell is like. It does, nevertheless, provide a number of
small glimpses that, when pieced together, reveal a gruesome
picture. We cannot know whether the statements made about
hell are meant as literal truths or as mere representations of
truth. Even if the latter is the case, it can only mean that the
facts they represent are so horrible that people simply couldn't
handle them. As you read these descriptions, please keep in
mind that most of them were given by the most loving Person
this world has ever encountered.

When most people think of hell, the first thing that comes to their mind is fire. It is with good reason. Jesus said that at the end of the age His angels will "…gather out of His kingdom all stumbling blocks, and those who commit lawlessness, and will throw them into the furnace of fire." (Matthew 13:41-42) He also said, "If your eye causes you to stumble, throw it out; it is better for you to enter the kingdom of God with one eye, than, having two eyes, to be cast into hell, where their worm does not die, and the fire is not quenched." (Mark 9:47-48) In yet another place, He told the story about the rich man in hell who pleaded for someone to "dip the tip of his finger in water and cool off my tongue, for I am in agony in this flame.'" (Luke 16:24) Isaiah apparently saw the place of the doomed and asked, "Who among us shall dwell with the devouring fire? Who among us shall dwell with everlasting burnings?" (Isaiah 33:14) John said, "If anyone worships the beast and his image, and receives a mark on his forehead or on his hand…he will be tormented with fire and brimstone in the presence of the holy angels and in the presence of the Lamb. And the smoke of their torment goes up forever and ever; they have no rest day and night…" (Revelation 14:10-11) And, of course, we are told that "if anyone's name was not found written in the book of life, he was thrown into the lake of fire." (Revelation 20:15)

Another metaphor Jesus used to describe this terrible place is outer darkness. (Matthew 8:12; 22:13; 25:30) Peter spoke of "pits of darkness" and "black darkness." (II Peter 2:4, 17) Albert Barnes wrote the following:

> It is not improbable that the image was taken from Roman dungeons or prisons. They were commonly constructed under ground. They were shut out from the light of the sun. They were, of course, damp, dark, and unhealthy, and probably most filthy…What a striking image

of future woe! Go to a damp, dark, solitary, and squalid dungeon; see a miserable and enraged victim; add to his sufferings the idea of eternity, and then remember that this, after all, is but an image, a faint image, of hell![6]

Jesus also mentioned the fact that these wretched souls would also be at the mercy of demonic tormentors. He said that the unforgiving servant would be handed "…over to the torturers until he should repay all that was owed him." (Matthew 18:34) In a different passage we read of the "…slave who knew his master's will and did not get ready or act in accord with his will, will receive many lashes…" (Luke 12:47-48) Yet another faithless slave will be cut "…in pieces and assign[ed] a place with the hypocrites; in that place there will be weeping and gnashing of teeth." (Matthew 24:51)

John Bunyan wrote an allegory in which he described some of the afflictions of hell. The following is a dialogue between a temporary visitor and a tormenting spirit. From this interchange one can imagine not only the suffering that goes on there daily but also why the person had to be sent there.

> *Fiend*: This is no more than a just retribution. In her lifetime, this woman was such a sordid wretch that though she had enough gold, she could never be satisfied. Therefore, now I pour it down her throat. She did not care who she ruined and undid so that she could get their gold. When she had amassed a greater treasure than she could ever spend, her love of money would not let her spend [it]…
>
> Since gold was her god on earth, is it not just that she should have her bellyful in hell?
>
> When her tormentor had finished speaking, I asked her whether what he said were true or not. To this, she answered me, "No, to my grief, it is not."

"How to your grief?" said I.

She answered: Because if what my tormentor tells you were true, I would be better satisfied. He tells you it is gold that he pours down my throat, but he is a lying devil and speaks falsely. If it were gold, I would never complain. But he abuses me, and instead of gold, he only gives me horrid, stinking sulfur. Had I my gold, I would still be happy. I value it so much that if I had it here, I scarcely would bribe heaven with it to be removed from here.[7]

Bunyan later shows the final end of false teachers as well.

Passing a little farther, we saw a multitude of damned souls together, gnashing their teeth with extreme rage and pain, while the tormenting fiends with hellish fury poured liquid fire and brimstone continually on them. In the meantime, they cursed God, themselves, and those about them, blaspheming after a fearful manner.

I could not help but ask of one fiend that so tormented them, who they were that he abused so cruelly.

Fiend: They are those who well deserve it...These are those souls who have been the great agents of hell on the earth and therefore deserve a particular regard in hell. We use our utmost diligence to give everyone his share of torments, but we will be sure to take care that these will not lack for punishment. These have not only their own sins to answer for, but also all those they have led astray, both by their doctrine and example.[8]

Another dreadful picture of hell that comes to me is seen in the *Lord of the Rings* trilogy,* where a hobbit named Smeagol

---

* I should make a personal note here. My wife and I have a TV set, but it has no antenna, cable or satellite connection. We typically watch a handful of DVD's a month. The *Lord of the Rings* series has been one of the few Hollywood movies we have been willing to view.

becomes so enthralled with the ring of Sauron that he kills another hobbit to get it. Little does he realize the price he will pay for his "Precious." He spends the next 500 years in an underground cavern growing increasingly obsessed with the ring and going insane. He emerges a hideous, deformed creature that is an outward expression of the corruption that has consumed his inner being.

This is only a movie; hell is real. However, it does illustrate what the Bible infers about lost sinners. The lust for sin will carry on into a person's eternity. Over time the rebel will probably suffer more from the madness and corrupting influences of his beloved sins than anything else.

One of the worst elements of hell will be the mental anguish sinners will face. Seven different times Jesus described hell as a place of "weeping and gnashing of teeth." (Matthew 8:12; 13:42: 13:50; 22:13; 24:51; 25:30; Luke 13:28) One can only imagine what it will be like for a person to be unable to do anything that would distract him from the agony. Not only does he retain his ability to think, but it seems as though his unencumbered mind will be able to think and feel much more clearly than while on earth.

Another aspect of this will be that he will remember everything about his life. In the story Jesus told about Lazarus and the rich man (Luke 16:19-31), there is a point when Abraham tells the wealthy man to "remember." What an enemy a person's memory will prove to be in hell!

On earth, there is much to crowd past memories out of one's consciousness. They lie dormant within the person's inner being like sunken ships resting on the ocean floor. They are there, even if they cannot now be perceived. It is an interesting phenomenon of the elderly that, while they often lose track of the mundane activities of the daily life, long lost memories from childhood vividly return.

What will the person remember? I'm sure that the scenes

played out on the screens of judgment will dance with tormenting regularity across his mind. Over and over again he will be reminded of his selfishness. Pictures of his many sinful deeds will etch themselves into his mind. All the different times he acted arrogantly will come in full view. Most of all, he will see how God had tried in vain to reach his hard and stubborn heart. "Oh, had I only listened! Had I only humbled myself!" The thoughts will plague him forever and ever.

Another picture of damnation is given by the Apostle Paul. He wrote, "For the wages of sin is death..." (Romans 6:23) and spoke of those who would "pay the penalty of eternal destruction, away from the presence of the Lord..." (II Thessalonians 1:9) Charles Finney offers the following fearful picture of what this means:

> When my last child died, the struggle was long; O, it was a fearfully protracted and agonizing twenty-four hours in the agonies of dissolving nature! It made me wish I could not see it! But suppose it had continued till this time. I should long since have died myself under the anguish and nervous exhaustion of witnessing such a scene. So would all our friends. Who could survive to the final termination of such an awful death? Who would not cry out, "My God, cut it short, cut it short in mercy!" When my wife died, her death-struggles were long and heart-rending. If you had been there, you would have cried mightily to God, "Cut it short! O, cut it short and relieve this dreadful agony!
> But suppose...a poor man cannot die! He lingers in the death agony a month, a year, five years, ten years till all his friends are broken down, and fall into their graves under the insupportable horror of the scene: but still the poor man cannot die! He outlives one generation then

another and another; one hundred years he is dying in mortal agony, and yet he comes no nearer to the end! What would you think of such a scene? It would be an illustration that is all a feeble illustration of the awful "second death!"

God would have us understand what an awful thing sin is, and what fearful punishment it deserves. He would fain show us by such figures how terrible must be the doom of the determined sinner...[9]

Whatever horrors await the lost soul, one thing is certain: he will have no hope of ever escaping. Once he has heard the pronouncement: "Depart from Me, accursed one" (Matthew 25:41), his doom has been sealed forever. Once the door has been shut, it will never again be opened.

Considering what we have just read, it is not difficult to understand why our loving Savior told His disciples, "My friends, do not be afraid of those who kill the body and after that have no more that they can do. I will warn you whom to fear: fear the One who, after He has killed, has authority to cast into hell; yes, I tell you, fear Him!" (Luke 12:4-5)

God has made every provision available for a person to be saved from this terrible doom. It is His good pleasure to offer salvation for "whosoever will." But the choice is ours. Will we offer an unconditional surrender to His Son? Or will we continue to go our own way?

Section Two:

THE GREAT APOSTASY

As we have seen, there have always been hypocrites attached to the Church. However, according to Scripture, the Church of the Last Days is characterized by its fallen condition. Hypocrisy isn't the occasional exception but the *norm*.

"The world is always pleased to rest in outward observances, and to substitute the form of godliness for the spirit. The devil knows that and gives them, in his gospel, a full supply."
∼ R. Hall[1]

"Until self-effacing men return again to spiritual leadership, we may expect a progressive deterioration in the quality of popular Christianity year after year till we reach the point where the grieved Holy Spirit withdraws—like the Shekinah from the temple." ∼ A.W. Tozer[2]

"The greatest threat to America today is not Communism, nor the Arab oil blackmail pressed upon us, nor the severe ecology crisis. The greatest threat to America today is GOD. God was married to Israel. He divorced Israel and has not bothered with her for 2,000 years. Why does He have to tolerate our sin? Can He not walk out on us?" ∼ Leonard Ravenhill[3]

Chapter Eight

THE RISE OF THE APOSTATE CHURCH

*"That day will not come except the apostasy comes
first [unless the predicted great falling away of those
who have professed to be Christians has come]."*
(II Thessalonians 2:3 AMP)

Although he is better known for his role on *The Love Boat*, Gavin MacLeod cited his supporting performance in the 2003 film *Time Changer* as "the most important thing" he had ever done. It's hard to disagree with him.

The storyline occurs in 1890 and revolves around Bible professor Russell Carlisle, who is unwittingly transported by a time machine into modern-day America. For five days, he finds himself trapped in a wicked world to which you and I have become shamefully accustomed.

In his day, the term, "Gay Nineties," referred to the nation's innocence, not to the filthy and lewd behavior reflected in our past decade. Men married their wives for life, with divorce rates hovering around a microscopic 5%. Teenage promiscuity, marital infidelity and abortion were almost nonexistent. Pornography—even if you could find it—was typically an artist's rendering of a topless woman.

Christian filmmaker Rich Christiano's character, Russell Carlisle, is an awkward and unlikely hero who is thrust into the

America of our day. This results in the inevitable scenes of him marveling over modern technology and dodging speeding cars. More important, though, are his reactions to the stark contrast in morality between the two eras.

At one point, he is seen watching television. His horrified expression betrays the fact that he is witnessing the kind of blatant immorality which has become standard fare for many of us. But perhaps the most poignant scene occurs when he is invited by some Christians to attend a movie with them. Suddenly, he is shown running out of the theater screaming at the employees, "You have to stop this movie! That actor took the Lord's name in vain! He blasphemed God!"

If you or I witnessed a fellow believer acting this way, our first thought would probably be, "What a nut case!" We would quickly distance ourselves from him. And yet this scenario provokes a few pointed questions Christians should ask themselves. Why aren't we more outraged when we hear actors take the Lord's name in vain? How can we look upon scantily-clad girls on television without blushing? Why do we permit TV to indoctrinate our children with the world's values? The answer to these questions is clear: we have given our culture a greater place in our lives than the Word of God. In short, we are corporately backslidden.

PREDICTIONS FROM ANOTHER TIME

One of the challenges of examining biblical prophecies about the Church in the end-times is that we are in the throes of it right now. We are engulfed in the spirit of the age and do not realize how much it influences our perspectives. To put it another way, "we can't see the forest for the trees." The only way to get a proper sight of a forest is to rise above it by taking a plane ride or climbing a nearby mountain. From that vantage point a person can scan the entire horizon, see the lay of hills, valleys and rivers and determine the best course through it.

The one who desires to "discern the signs of the times" also needs a view from the outside. One effective way of acquiring that objective perspective is to consider what writers from yesteryear saw pertaining to the end of the age. It is true that today's teachers can "connect the dots" in ways that old-time writers couldn't. They are witnesses of things that would have seemed inconceivable a century ago: atomic weaponry, Israel as a nation, microchips implanted under the skin, computer systems able to track and manage mankind, etc. Writers from past centuries didn't have that knowledge at their disposal. Instead, they relied on the Holy Spirit to illumine Scripture about what the end-times would look like for Christians. In other words, they weren't attempting to make Bible verses coincide with their opinions about what was happening around them.

Take Matthew Henry (1662-1714) for instance. When he studied the passage in Second Thessalonians 2 about the Great Apostasy, he saw it as a defection "from sound doctrine, instituted worship…and a holy life. The apostle speaks of some very great apostasy…such as should be very general, though gradual…"[4] He apparently believed this falling away would be very difficult to discern because it would creep into the Church over a period of time. It is the old "frog in the kettle" syndrome; i.e., the frog is oblivious to the fact that he is being cooked because the water in the kettle is heating up so slowly. When Mr. Henry considered the inconceivable reality that the majority of Christians would abandon the Truth, he surmised that this could only happen slowly and gradually.

He also saw it as being "general" in nature. In other words, he predicted that the apostasy would be widespread and extensive. This was not going to be a minor segment of the Church but a large percentage; it was going to be the norm, not the exception. Beloved, does that frighten you? It should!

Albert Barnes (1798-1870) saw a direct correlation of the Great

Apostasy with the spiritual climate Paul described in Second Timothy 3.* He wrote: "It shall be one of the characteristics of those times that men shall be eminently selfish—evidently under the garb of religion…no one can doubt the correctness of the prophecy of the apostle that it would exist 'in the last times.'…This shows that the apostle referred to some great corruption in the church; and there can be little doubt that he had his eye on the same great apostasy to which he refers in 2 Thes. 2. and 1 Tim. 4…He saw the 'germ' of what was yet to grow up into so gigantic a system of iniquity as to overshadow the world."[5]

Paul's words about pervasive self-centeredness offer a prime example of the adage: "we can't see the forest for the trees." Most of us in the U.S. have grown up in prosperity and have never known anything different. Although there have always been self-centered people, it has probably never been seen on the scale we have today in America. However, because we have grown up this way it seems normal to us. But there is a reason Jesus spoke of "the deceitfulness of riches." (Mark 4:19) Indeed, we have been corporately deceived and now obliviously pursue our self-centered lives.

Barnes envisioned this selfishness bringing about a "great corruption" within the Church and growing into a "gigantic system of iniquity." There is a true Church alive within the United States, but make no mistake about this: it lies within a false religious system that has taken root in our country and has spread around the world.

Pulpit Commentator A.C. Hervey (c. 1890) also saw Second Timothy 3 as a description of the apostasy: "Characteristics of the apostasy. The doctrinal degeneracy is marked by a widespread moral decay…They prefer the friendship of the world to the friendship of God. Thus, the long catalogue of moral enormity

---

* "But realize this, that in the last days difficult times will come. For men will be lovers of self…" (II Timothy 3:1-2a)

developed by the apostasy began with 'the love of self,' and ends with 'the love of pleasure,' to the utter exclusion, first and last, of the 'love of God.'"[6]

If Christian pollsters are correct in their assumptions, millions of evangelical men are addicted to pornography. Hervey's words about "widespread moral decay" makes one wonder if he took his own time journey from 1890 to 21st Century America! What would this man think if he came into our time and saw professing Christians regularly viewing images of people involved in aberrant sex? Could he possibly have been any more accurate when he saw the great falling away beginning with "the love of self" and reaching its climax in "the love of pleasure?"

Then there is the old-time Puritan, John Owens (1616-1683), who saw three prevailing characteristics of the Last Days. First, "the profession of true religion is outwardly maintained under a visible predominance of horrible lusts and wickedness."[7] Wow! Do you realize what it must have meant for a Puritan of the 1600's to envision masses of professing Christians dominated by an insatiable appetite for uncleanness? Somehow—and it surely must have been a great mystery to him—he saw this occurring openly in the Church.

The second thing he saw was a time when "men are prone to forsake the truth, and seducers abound to gather them up."[8] This great deception is so prevalent in the eschatological writings of the New Testament that it is not surprising he would see it as a major spiritual development.

The third thing he saw was professing Christians "mixing themselves with the world, and learning their manner."[9] A.C. Hervey wrote essentially the same thing: "They prefer the friendship of the world to the friendship of God." Both of these men fully expected worldliness to be one of the principal features of the end-times Church.

How could any sincere person deny this fact? Christians

indulge the lust of the flesh like never before through countless forms of pleasure (indulgent eating, viewing pornography, abusing drugs, etc.) and entertainment (following sports, playing video games, viewing television, etc.). American churchgoers have the financial means to give themselves nearly any possession for which their eyes lust. Prideful ambition is driving people to ever greater heights of outward success and prominence. Yes, evangelicals are fully engulfed in a love for "the things of the world" and are seemingly oblivious to the fact that their "love for the Father" has grown ice cold. They can claim to love God, but their daily lives are a denial of it. Surely these predictions are unfolding right before our eyes!

THE GREAT APOSTASY

What exactly is the Great Apostasy? Apparently, in the days just before the return of Christ, there will be[†] a massive movement away from a true, intimate relationship with Christ. In the passage of Scripture where Paul warned about the powerful nature of the deception which would accompany the Antichrist, he also said that our "gathering together to" Jesus would not occur "unless the apostasy comes first..." (II Thessalonians 2:3)

The word apostasy (Gk. *apostasia*) is actually only used twice in the New Testament. *Strong's Bible Dictionary* defines it as a "defection from truth... falling away, forsake." The *International Standard Bible Encyclopedia* goes into a little more depth: "a standing away from, a falling away, a withdrawal, a defection... abandonment of the faith." The *Vine's Word Dictionary* says, "a defection, revolt...to forsake...used politically of rebels."

When speaking of an individual, apostasy means to abandon a relationship with God that a person once had. But regarding God's people in general, the term should actually be broadened.

---

† The point of this book is to prove that we are in the throes of it right now.

The Christian Church is the depository of God's Spirit. When a major segment of that body of people lives in hypocrisy, it could be said that the Church has experienced apostasy.

It should also be noted that this Greek word can be used not only to describe those who forsake religious beliefs but also applies to those who rebel against authority. Today's rejection of God's authority in the lives of many professing Christians certainly must be considered a part of this great falling away.

While there is a smattering of statements throughout the Bible about this terrible event, I believe there are five particular sections of Scripture‡ where the spiritual climate within the Church is described in detail. We will examine these passages throughout the second half of this book. The Greek terms utilized by the biblical writers are key to understanding what is taking place and what is to come.

Let's take a moment right now to look at Jesus' Last Days Discourse found in Matthew 24-25. After laying a foundation by describing worldwide events, He then shifted His attention to what will be happening in the Church:

> And at that time many will *fall away* (Gk. *skandalizo*) and will betray one another and hate one another. And many false prophets will arise, and will *mislead* (Gk. *planao*) many. Because lawlessness is increased, most people's love will grow cold. But the one who endures to the end, he will be saved. (Matthew 24:10-13)

Jesus employed two Greek terms in this passage that warrant a closer examination. The first is *skandalizo*, which the NASB translates as *fall away*. Look at the usage of this phrase in some other translations:

‡ Matthew 24-25; II Thessalonians 2; II Timothy 3:1-4:4; II Peter 2-3; and Revelation 17-18. It should be noted that, from the eternal perspective, secular history is of little importance and really only acts as a backdrop to God's interactions with His people. The Church is central in any discussion the Bible may have about the Last Days.

- And then many will be offended and repelled and will begin to distrust and desert [*Him Whom they ought to trust and obey*] and will stumble and fall away…(AMP)
- And numbers of people will be turned from the right way…(BBE)
- Many will give up their faith at that time…(GNB)
- Then many people will fall by the way…(ISV)
- And many will turn away from [Jesus]…(NLT)
- Then comes the time when many will lose their faith…(PHP)

The best commentary one can find on Matthew 24:10 is when Jesus talked about those with "rocky soil" in the parable of the Sower and the Seed. He said, "…when they hear the word, immediately [they] receive it with joy; and they have no firm root in themselves, but are only temporary; then, when affliction or persecution arises because of the word, immediately they fall away (*skandalizo*)." (Mark 4:16-17)

Applying this biblical truth to the climate of the Last Days, Jesus is saying that there will be many who will gladly follow Him—until their faith costs them something! When things become difficult they will desert Him *en masse*. Also, take note of the word *temporary*. This does not necessarily apply only to those who fall away from the faith after a few months; it can also describe those who have professed Christ for many years but whose faith has never really been tested.

The second important term Jesus used is *planao*, translated variously in the NASB as *mislead* (Matthew 24:24), *gone astray* (Matthew 18:12) and *deceives* (Revelation 12:9). The Amplified Bible translates Matthew 24:11: "And many false prophets will rise up and deceive and lead many into error." Jesus actually used this word four different times during this teaching. (Matthew 24:4, 5, 11, 24) I think He was trying to tell us something! Not only did He alert us to this great deception, but Paul also warned about falsehood during the end of the age. Only a fool would read such urgent warnings about deception with a careless attitude. Beloved, you and I are vulnerable to being deceived! This deception is massive. *Many* are falling away, but the deception is that they don't realize it is happening to them. They honestly believe that they are walking with the Lord.

We will discuss this subject in more detail later in the book, but can you see how far we have corporately drifted from the godly atmosphere that was in the Church a century ago? If "Russell Carlisle" stepped into our Christian world today, he would not feel at home. He would see it for what it really is: the Apostate Church that Jesus and Paul both described.

Surely, for the sincere believer, these are "perilous times of great stress and trouble [*hard to deal with and hard to bear*]." (II Timothy 3:1 AMP) As my friend Jim Ruddy points out: "The only other time this word *perilous* (Gk. *chalepos*) is used is in Matthew 8:28 where it is referring to the *violence* of the Gadarene demoniac. My paraphrase has always been that the Last Days will be demon-driven days!" Little wonder the Lord asked, "When the Son of Man comes, will He find faith on the earth?" (Luke 18:8)

"To save your life in self-centered concern is to lose it, and to lose it in Self-surrender is to find it."
ᔓ E. Stanley Jones[1]

"Before we can be clean and ready for Him to control, self-seeking, self-glory, self-interest, self-pity, self-righteousness, self-importance, self-promotion, self-satisfaction—and whatsoever else there be of self—must die
ᔓ Leonard Ravenhill[2]

"By nature the throne-place, our heart, is quite fully occupied with self. And self does not want God to rule as king, but only to serve as a slave-servant." ᔓ Rex Andrews[3]

"The way of the world is self seeking and self-shielding. 'Spare thyself' is the sum of its philosophy. But the doctrine of Christ is not 'save thyself' but sacrifice thyself. There is no such thing as belonging to Christ and living to please self. Make no mistake on that point."
ᔓ A. W. Pink[4]

Chapter Nine:
SPIRIT OF THE AGE

"For people will be lovers of self and [utterly]
self-centered, proud and arrogant and contemptuous
boasters. They will be inflated with self-conceit."
(II Timothy 3:2, 4 AMP)
"...and because of the prevalent disregard of God's
law the love of the great majority will grow cold."
(Matthew 24:12 WNT)

I grew up as a typical, suburban Baby Boomer of the 1960's. Little affection was shown in my home, which seemed to create in me an inordinate degree of self-centeredness. As a spoiled child I received nearly every toy I demanded. Self-love was already beginning to establish itself as the ruling principle of my young life.

When I entered my teenage years, I discovered sex, which would prove to be the real love of my life. For the next 12 years I gave myself over to the pursuit of it. I manipulated scores of girls into giving up their bodies and became increasingly addicted to pornography. Self-gratification became my entire life. My world shrank to the point that I had no room for anyone else. I remember once having the conscious thought that I would never do anything unless there was something in it for me. People were only a means to some end. The selfish little boy who demanded the latest toys had grown into a lust-driven monster.

When I became a believer, the Lord immediately set to work on disassembling the enormous structure of self-centeredness

that I had erected within. I had so trained myself to "look out for number one," that I could hardly even comprehend what it meant to do something for someone else without receiving something in return.

The first fifteen years of ministry were, for the most part, extremely painful. The Lord severely chastened me to teach me to obey Him. He had to plunge the scalpel deep to carve the poison of sin out of my heart. Time and again He was forced to overthrow various idols that were still thriving in my bosom. Those years produced countless episodes of heart-wrenching repentance. I had to pay a great price to be freed from the prison of Self that once held me bound.

I could easily have been a poster child for the "Me Generation." Most of us who have been raised since the 1960's have never known what it really means to do without. We have grown up in a level of prosperity the world has never before known.

A couple of statistics I recently read say much about the U.S. lifestyle. The living standard of the average welfare recipient in America ranks within the middle class of the other top 10 countries of the world; our poorest people live better than the middle-class folks of over 240 other nations. The second stat states that the average American cat eats better than at least one billion people on our planet—people just like you and me!

In the U.S., we enjoy a more opulent lifestyle—full of luxury, pleasure, and comfort—than many kings down through world history. No monarch from past centuries ever enjoyed indoor plumbing, electricity, television, newspapers, toasters, automobiles, ambulance service, telephones and all of the other things that we now consider to be absolute necessities. Yesterday's luxuries have become today's necessities. Recent examples include cell phones and personal computers. It wasn't that long ago that only the rich could afford such devices. Now, nearly every American has both.

This tremendous prosperity tends to keep people in a constant state of wanting more. Moreover, advertisers do a remarkable job of training us to never be satisfied. Everywhere we look we are being told about some new item that we just *cannot* live without. Clothes, computers, cars, vacations, houses and furniture are paraded before us to keep us in a fixed state of covetousness: always lusting for more, we are never satisfied.

There is no question that our culture has become increasingly self-centered. We have been taught to see ourselves as the center of everything: what *I* want, where *I* want to go, what makes *me* feel good, what fulfills *me*. "The very air you breathe is a poisonous fume"* of selfishness. We have corporately achieved the great American dream and it has left us miserable and unfulfilled. Surely the spirit of the age in which we live is *self-centeredness*. Self-love rules the day.

THE CHRISTIAN LIFE

It should go without saying that looking out for one's needs and personal interests is a natural part of life. Every person endeavors to improve his lot in life. No one in his right mind desires suffering or deprivation; on the contrary, it is normal to long for happiness, comfort and security. It is part of the make-up of the human being to protect one's own life and interests. Paul attested to this fact when he wrote, "No one ever hated his own flesh, but nourishes and cherishes it…" (Ephesians 5:29)

However, a new craving wells up from within when the Holy Spirit takes residence in a new believer's heart. God is not a taker but a giver, and so when a person is truly converted his "ruling principle" begins to undergo a transformation. Paul touched on this new way of life when he wrote, "Do nothing from selfishness or empty conceit, but with humility of mind regard one another as more important than yourselves; do not

---

* A phrase referring to Mordor from *The Fellowship of the Ring*.

merely look out for your own personal interests, but also for the interests of others. Have this attitude in yourselves which was also in Christ Jesus." (Philippians 2:3-5)

It is interesting that nearly everything the Bible puts forward as strengthening one's Christian life is directly opposite to that which the flesh desires. Real prayer can be very exhausting. Studying and meditating on Scripture is much more difficult than reading a newspaper or watching *Good Morning America*. And, of course, fasting is downright disagreeable!

Jesus brought to light a very important truth about Christianity when He said, "If you love those who love you, what credit is that to you? For even sinners love those who love them." (Luke 6:32) Jesus was making the point that there should be something much different about the life of a believer. His life should stand out from the unsaved around him.

True believers "become partakers of the divine nature." (II Peter 1:4) What else could explain the long history of self*less*ness that has been the hallmark of Christianity down through the centuries? Think about those who chose to be mauled and eaten alive by wild animals in the Coliseum rather than deny their Savior. Consider the saintly people who endured the torture racks of the Inquisition because they refused to betray other believers. What about those who preferred to be burned alive at the stake rather than give up their belief that people had a right to read the Scriptures? It was also not that long ago that sadistic Communists committed horrible atrocities against believers. Even today Christians in various countries are being put to death for their faith. Truly, there have been multitudes martyred for the name of Christ.

Nevertheless, it would be a mistake to romanticize these people's lives. They were normal folks like you and me. Each one of them had once been wholly consumed with their own interests. The only way they could go through such suffering was because their lives had been so affected by God. Not every believer is forced to suffer martyrdom or persecution, but every follower of Christ is expected to renounce his Self-life and serve other people in some capacity.

The Apostle Paul certainly had this testimony. His entire youth was devoted to becoming a leader among the Pharisees. He was utterly Self-righteous and Self-absorbed. He had such an ugly, hateful spirit that he threw himself into "ravaging the church." (Acts 8:3) By his own admission he had been "a blasphemer and a persecutor and a violent aggressor." (I Timothy 1:13) He eventually met Christ on a dusty Syrian road and then spent the final 30 years of his life living for Him. The reality of Christ in his life is seen by the power of God at work in his dealings with others and in his willingness to suffer for his Savior. This was the Christian life to which Paul had become accustomed.

END-TIMES CHURCH

The "Apostle to the Gentiles" was probably in his sixties when he was arrested for the final time. Nero had just begun burning Christians alive and throwing them to the lions in the Coliseum. As a Roman citizen, Paul could not be tortured, but this was not the case for most of his fellow Christian inmates. I'm sure he regularly witnessed deeds of great moral courage in that prison.

As Paul sat in that Roman prison cell awaiting execution, he wrote one final letter to his assistant Timothy. He was in the process of sharing some final instructions to his beloved disciple when a string of prophetic thoughts unexpectedly began to flow into his mind about the Church of the Last Days. What came to him must have been shocking and terribly disconcerting. During that crucial time before the return of Christ, the prevailing characteristic of His people would not be the kind of self*less*ness he was seeing around him; it would be just the opposite! As inexplicable as it must have seemed to him, professing Christians would be known for their selfishness, pride and sin. Their hearts would not be passionate about the things of God but the passing pleasures of this world. I believe he was seeing 21st Century American Christianity.†

We've already talked about the Self-absorbed culture in which we live. And one would expect unbelievers to pursue with gusto everything that they fancy. But is it really any different for those who claim to be Christian? For instance, of the 50,000 thoughts we entertain in any given day, how many revolve around the things of God? How many are centered on meeting the needs of those whom He loves? The truth is that most people spend the bulk of their time thinking about what they want, what they like, what they are interested in and what they want to do.

Self-love can take a thousand different forms in the life of a churchgoer. For the struggler with sin, it is found in his obsession with his beloved idol. For the religious man, Self manifests itself in rigid formalism, denominational pride, doctrinal narrowness or simply seeing himself as better than others. A narcissist enjoys talking about himself during his weekly meetings with his counselor. Someone else loves being the center of attention at church. This total absorption with Self can also be seen at the local Christian bookstore where the preponderance of books focus on what God wants to do for the believer. *It isn't Christ who is the center of American Christianity but man.* Yes, Self-love rules in the Church as well.

It should go without saying that Self-love is the exact opposite of the unselfishness which characterizes God's kingdom. The Greek term *agape* expresses the prevailing passion found in the great heart of God. Jesus said the greatest commandment was to "love (*agape*) the Lord your God with all your heart, and with

---

† As the leading Christian nation, we have exported our selfish gospel to free Christians around the world.

all your soul, and with all your mind." (Matthew 22:37) His point was that all of the affections of one's heart should be directed toward God; every other relationship paling in comparison. One's entire life (Gk. *psuche*, translated variously as *soul* and *life*) should be devoted to the things God considers important. One's mind should be utterly absorbed in the Lord.

This union with God produces a love that in turn flows out to other people. Christians are called to be receptacles, possessors and dispensers of that love. Every true believer understands what it means to get out of his "comfort zone" to help those who are in need. *Agape* love *must* extend itself. The Holy Spirit dwelling within a believer *must* find someone to channel His love toward.

A Self-based religion does not have or require this level of commitment. Self-centered people cannot fathom possessing such devotion to God or giving themselves to other people like this. C.S. Lewis shows the small-mindedness and the inevitable end of those who will not give themselves to others:

> To love at all is to be vulnerable. Love anything, and your heart will certainly be wrung and possibly be broken. If you want to make sure of keeping it intact, you must give your heart to no one not even to an animal. Wrap it carefully round with hobbies and little luxuries; avoid all entanglements; lock it up safe in the casket or coffin of your selfishness. But in that casket—safe, dark motionless, airless—it will change. It will not be broken; it will become unbreakable, impenetrable, irredeemable. The alternative to tragedy, or at least to the risk of tragedy, is damnation. The only place outside Heaven where you can be perfectly safe from all the dangers and perturbations of love is Hell...
>
> Every Christian would agree that a man's spiritual health is exactly proportional to his love for God.[5]

When Jesus gave His discourse about the Last Days, He made one simple statement regarding *agape* in the Church.‡ He said, "Because lawlessness is increased, most people's love (*agape*) will grow cold." (Matthew 24:12) In other words, because people would learn to treat God's commandments with disdain, they would not be able to abide in His love. Deep affection for the Lord and the passion to help others would gradually become swallowed up in ugly selfishness.

The sad and tragic fact is that He was not referring to the unbelievers of the world; the context of His statements is plainly referring to professing Christians. Moreover, His use of the word "most" clearly shows that this lovelessness would be the prevailing climate throughout the end-times Church.

Jesus concluded His remarks about Christians with the statement, "But the one who endures to the end, he will be saved." (Matthew 24:13) Was He telling Christians to store up canned goods and hunker down through the Tribulation period? No; He was saying that those believers who spend the rest of their lives in love with God and actively living out that love by laying down their lives for others—regardless of what is occurring on earth—will find salvation at the end of their road.

FOSTERING THE PRIDE OF LIFE

There is another form that Self-love can take within a person's heart. It is the perspective a person holds of himself in relation to God and other people. The common term used to describe this form of Self-love is pride. And according to the Apostle Paul, this fallen passion would be prevalent in the Apostate Church. (II Timothy 3:2, 4)

---

‡ If you recall, this is one of the five sections of Scripture I mentioned in Chapter Eight where the spiritual climate within the Church is described in detail. Matthew 24 mostly describes what life is like on planet earth just prior to His return. However, He also intersperses comments about professing Christians throughout the chapter. Verses 9-13 are a direct commentary on the Church during that time.

Unfortunately, most believers' perspective of pride is so superficial that it makes them oblivious to its presence in their own lives. They can easily identify it in swaggering Hollywood actors, snooty rich people, egotistical sports stars or even a loud-mouthed co-worker. But ask them if *they* struggle with being prideful and most likely denial will kick in right away. "Oh, no! Not me!" What contemporary pastor has ever had an anxious church member come into his office lamenting over his struggles with pride?

Whether or not we recognize its odious presence, pride lurks within every human heart. It is a corrosive agent that permeates our fallen nature and eats away at one's soul if left undetected. Indeed, there is much within the human heart that exalts itself against God. (II Corinthians 10:5)

The Bible certainly leaves no doubt as to what God's position is on pride. Solomon said that "a proud look" is an abomination to the Lord. (Proverbs 6:17) Jesus said, "…whoever exalts himself shall be humbled…" (Matthew 23:12) James said, "God is opposed to the proud…" (James 4:6) In Psalms, the Lord Himself said, "Whoever has haughty eyes and a proud heart, him will I not endure." (Psalm 101:5b NIV)

Unquestionably, pride is one of the most prominent subjects addressed in Scripture. The Bible uses at least 17 different words (and countless derivatives) to describe this spiritual disease.§ However, no matter which term is used, there is almost always a connotation of height: something high, rising, exalted or being lifted up. Thus, a proud person has a high estimation of himself and lifts himself above those around him. This concept of Self-exaltation forms the basis for our working definition of pride: *Having an exaggerated sense of one's own importance and a selfish preoccupation with one's own rights.* It is the attitude that says, "I am

---

§ For instance, in one sentence Jeremiah uses several terms to describe Moab: "We have heard of the pride (*ga'own*) of Moab—he is very proud (*ge'eh*)—of his haughtiness (*gobahh*), his pride (*ga'own*), his arrogance (*ga'own*) and his Self-exaltation (*ruwm*)." (Jeremiah 48:29)

more important than you and, if need be, I will promote my cause and protect my rights at your expense."

Pride is the governing principle of hell and the unredeemed world it influences. It causes strife in the home, the workplace, the political arena and yes, even the Christian community. (Proverbs 13:10) Pride incites fierce competition among people in all facets of life. Without a doubt, it has caused more problems, conflicts, suffering and heartache on this earth than any other human passion. Every bit of it reeks with the ugly and selfish attitude of "taking care of number one."

Pride in America

The American culture is pregnant with the pride of life. Female beauty is glorified from coast to coast. Physical prowess in sports is given unprecedented acknowledgement. Human ingenuity in science and technology is exalted. Corporate greed is vaunted as shrewd investing. Politicians are praised—not for their integrity—but for pragmatism. Unmistakably, we are under the Darwinian curse of the survival of the fittest.

A few days after the terrorist attack on the World Trade Center, Florida Governor Jeb Bush, inflated with national pride, expressed the sentiments of most Americans when he said, "The aim of the terrorists is clear—to hurt and to humble America. They've indeed hurt us, but they will never humble us."¶ National unity was trumpeted with such statements as, "We are proud to be Americans!"

Almost everything in our culture caters to and incites man's pride: entertainment, advertising, the media, academics, business and the home life. Now more than ever, it's all about image and personal achievement. This, in turn, has created an

---

¶ The Governor's statement can be accessed at http://www.wavsource.com/news/20010911. htm. Of course, my comments here are not meant to infer that there is anything wrong with expressing patriotism about our nation.

overwhelming pressure to out-do the next man—to be smarter, stronger, more capable, more attractive and wealthier.

In such an environment that exalts and glorifies achievement, strength and beauty, it doesn't take long for children to learn that it feels good to be praised and hurts to be unnoticed or criticized. They are taught to be proud of who they are and of their abilities. This mentality is reinforced at every stage of development and throughout adulthood.

Take school for instance. As a means of motivation, the first thing teachers appeal to in a child is his pride by sending the message that if he wants to be rewarded by the system, he must *strive* to be the best. He must *out-do* others. He must show a *competitive* spirit. From a biblical perspective, each of these terms is a devilish manifestation of pride.

Early on in life, ambition and vainglory are instilled in children and are considered acceptable motives for doing their best.** Teachers attempt to awaken and stir up the pride that is already inherent in every child. Rather than teaching them godly principles that promote the importance of others, kids are taught that their value comes from *excelling* others. Competition becomes the means to induce young people to do the best they can do. They are encouraged to put themselves in the position of receiving man's applause no matter what the cost. They are told to be content with nothing less than the highest distinction. Our country is a country of winners. Losers are second-rate citizens.†† Therefore, a person's value is often determined by achievement rather than by moral character.

If a young man shows an interest in some profession, he

** It goes without saying that a parent or teacher *ought to* do their utmost to inspire children to do their best. Kids *should be* encouraged to put value in the quality of their work. They are *supposed to* urge young people to become accomplished in a field of interest. However, the current practice of measuring kids against each other to motivate them is not only unnecessary but is dangerous.

†† Some in the field of academics attempt to correct this through humanistic methods, e.g., refusing to fail a child who has not met the minimal scholastic requirements.

is taught to emulate successful people in his field: study their lives, imitate their practices and follow in their footsteps. And above all else, this determination to be the top in his field must be accompanied by a positive mental attitude. What glorious things await those who refuse to settle for second best!

Unbelievably, this same mentality is even thrust upon those training for the ministry. Godly characteristics such as love, humility and kindness tend to be impatiently brushed aside in favor of the outward signs of success. It is nearly always the most talented preachers who are put on a pedestal. Therefore, our young people aspire to imitate those with the biggest churches, the most popular radio shows, the best selling books and the most prestigious positions. Bible school students quickly learn that the evangelical system in America richly rewards its darlings. This worldly mindset permeates much of the Church in the United States.

In the current Church culture, if you want to be respected and admired, you must perform in such a way as to attract to yourself the most admirers. Surely, it is exactly as Paul predicted it would be: "For people will be lovers of self and [*utterly*] self-centered...proud and arrogant and contemptuous boasters...They will be...inflated with self conceit." (II Timothy 3:2, 4 AMP)

False teachers and carnal leaders may revel in the limelight for a time, but we are moving toward a day when man will be put in his place, once and for all. "The proud look of man will be abased and the loftiness of man will be humbled, and the Lord alone will be exalted in that day." (Isaiah 2:11)

"Man's carnal mind relishes a religion like that of the apostate Church, which gives an opiate to conscience, while leaving the sinner license to indulge his lusts."
— Jamieson, Fausset, Brown Commentary[1]

"An atheist once said, 'You can keep your heaven and your hell. Only give me this earth.' We may not dare to voice that, but do we live it with our lives? When the church begins to backslide, the first visible sign is usually an increase in worldliness...What crept ashamedly into the church before begins to walk in freely...Instead of walking in opposite directions, the world and the church begin to have more in common with each other." — Joel R. Beeke[2]

"If you choose to persist in pursuing worldly objects, it will prove that you are lovers of pleasure more than lovers of God; nay, that you are irreconcilably God's enemies."
— E. Payson[3]

Chapter Ten:
LOVERS OF PLEASURE

"They will be lovers of sensual pleasures and
vain amusements more than and rather
than lovers of God." (II Timothy 3:4 AMP)

I t should be understood at the outset that pleasure has its
rightful place in our lives. However, problems arise when
it is given more importance in a believer's daily life than
what is proper and allowable.

Making pleasure the most important aspect of one's life
could be compared to a teenager who thinks he can live on
candy bars and soda pop. True, he won't drop dead within a
few days on such an unhealthy diet, but his quality of life will be
seriously impaired. The constant intake of sugar will gradually
rot his teeth, deplete his overall energy level and could even
lead to something serious such as diabetes. Worse than that, by
substituting sweets for healthy food, his body will not receive
the nutrition that is required to ward off sickness and to sustain
life. Undoubtedly, the results of such a lifestyle would be a sickly
life and an untimely death.

In the same way, pleasurable experiences are meant to be the
dessert of life. Kept in proper perspective, they are balanced by
the staples of a healthy spiritual diet of prayer, Bible reading,

church attendance, deeds of kindness, giving of tithes and offerings, and so on. However, when gratification becomes the focal point of one's daily existence, it not only rots a person's spiritual life, but it eventually chokes out everything that is wholesome. It also dulls our spiritual senses and keeps our focus on worldly, temporal things rather than on the eternal values of God's kingdom. Even "good things" can take our focus away from God.

Jesus said that the love of pleasure chokes out the Word of God. (Luke 8:14) James told his constituents that their love for pleasure thwarted their prayers and kept them in a spirit of lust. (James 4:1-3) The writer of Hebrews held Moses up as an example to us all when he said that he chose "rather to endure ill-treatment with the people of God, than to enjoy the passing pleasures of sin." (Hebrews 11:25) The Apostle Paul spoke of those who are "enslaved to various lusts and pleasures." (Titus 3:3)

While these passages are each uniquely profound, it is Paul's prophetic words in Second Timothy 3:4 that are most alarming. There the Apostle speaks of those alive in the Last Days who would be "lovers of pleasure rather than lovers of God."

The sobering truth is, when seeking pleasure becomes the emphasis in one's life, a person's love for God begins to die. The desire for worldly pleasures nullifies one's ability to be in a true, loving relationship with God.

THE WORLD OF ENTERTAINMENT

Americans are serious about their amusements. In fact, we have become so addicted to entertainment that we cannot conceive of life without it. Americans play cards, board games, golf, baseball, soccer and football. They go swimming, biking, bowling, boating and fishing. They go to the movies, the beach, amusement parks, shopping malls and outlet centers. They read newspapers, magazines, romance novels, and tabloids; surf the Internet, visit chat rooms, rent movies, play video games and spend endless hours sitting in front of a television screen. In short, there is no end to our indulgences when it comes to entertainment.

In 2005, U.S. citizens purchased 1.43 billion movie tickets and 600 million music CD's. We spent $27 billion on video games, $22.4 billion on magazine subscriptions, $24 billion on books, $50 billion on gambling and $23.4 billion on buying and renting DVD's. 190 million of us have cell phones, while 69 million homes subscribe to cable TV. The grand total amount spent by Americans that year on these *legal* forms of entertainment is $199 billion, or approximately $721 for every man, woman and child. Obviously that number goes much higher when other unnamed forms of entertainment are added in—not to mention the multitude of illicit activities that could be included.[4]

As far as I have been able to tell, there are very few Christian homes that stand outside this massive indulgence in entertainment. The prevailing attitude seems to be that it is a Christian's right to watch television, play video games and go to the movies. God would not expect His children to—gasp!—live without some form of nightly amusement!

Surely, even the most jaded Christian would admit that television has become a source of continuous filth. Eight out of every ten primetime TV shows contain suggestive sexual content today, averaging five sex scenes per hour.[5] These are not quick snippets of bathing suits or couched comments about sexual matters, either. Primetime offerings and situation comedies (sit-coms) almost continually revolve around sexual storylines involving teenage promiscuity, extra-marital affairs, homosexuality and worse. Passionate sex scenes (sans open nudity) have become commonplace as well on daytime soap operas. Even televised sporting events are a vehicle for sleazy commercials which take direct aim at the sexual lust in men.

"Well, I know TV has a lot of junk on it," coos the

unrepentant Christian viewer, "but I'm careful about what I watch. If something questionable comes on, I just change the channel. Besides, what would I do at night if I couldn't watch TV?" This is the typical justification one hears from those who insist on viewing television in spite of its decadent fare.

Any sincere believer who truly has his priorities in order would find even the occasional swear word, sexual inference or near nudity as being unacceptable. (Where, oh where are the Russell Carlisle's of our generation?) But when someone is bent on having what he wants—in spite of the clear-cut consequences it brings—there is no talking him out of it. He will simply find a way to justify his actions.

What is particularly troubling to me is the callousness parents have over the way their children are affected by television. Consider some of the following facts.

The average time kids spend watching TV each day is four hours.[6] In fact, according to one study, they spend more time watching television than any other activity except sleep.[7] Over half of American kids have a television in their bedroom where they can watch it free of parental control.[8]

Children are not showing discernment about what they watch, either. For instance, Nielsen Ratings estimated that nearly 14 million kids (nearly half under the age of 12) were watching when Janet Jackson exposed her breast during the 2004 Super Bowl half-time show. They also stated that the most popular broadcast-network television show with kids aged 9-12 is ABC's *Desperate Housewives*.[9]

Children are not only being influenced in the realm of sexuality, but they are also receiving a regular dosage of violence. According to the American Psychiatric Association, the typical American youth will have seen 16,000 simulated murders and 200,000 acts of violence by the age of 18. They went on to say that children who have watched violent shows are more likely to strike out at playmates, argue, disobey authority and are less willing to wait for things.[10]

It is true that not every child who regularly views sexual situations or violent episodes on TV is going to go out and engage in the behavior they have just viewed. But it is sheer delusion to think that their perspectives and the choices they make in life are not being heavily influenced. It seems that every generation of Christian children raised on TV has become increasingly harder toward the things of God. I can't help but wonder how much all of this contributes to the fact that a large percentage of evangelical high school students stop attending church after they graduate.

What is inconceivable to me is the fact that Christian parents show such little concern over these facts. It seems that many churchgoers are so bent on having television they are willing to pay nearly any price for it—even the souls of their children.

Unfortunately, the deception and denial run deep and people become downright angry when one raises questions about their addiction to TV. For instance, in the early 1990's I was interviewed by the late Dr. D. James Kennedy on his radio program, *Truths That Transform.* The subject of the show that day was the effect television was having on the homes of Christians. One of the points I raised was that while people are faithfully bringing their children to church for 2-3 hours a week, they are also entrusting the minds of their kids to the godless culture of Hollywood for 20-40 hours a week. "Should they be surprised," I asked, "when their children go after other forms of pleasure this pagan culture offers such as promiscuity or drugs?" The producer later told me they received more complaints about that program than any other they had ever done. This reaction only proves to me that I hit a raw nerve with the Christian public that day.

MODERATION

As I have already stated, pleasure generally has its rightful place in our lives. It is true that God is happy to see His children enjoying the simple pleasures of life. However, most people are not content to keep it in its proper place; they want a lot of it and they want it often. Nevertheless, it is wise to show restraint in pursuing the amusements our culture offers.

Even innocent entertainment becomes sinful when it is overindulged. Let's say that you enjoy watching old reruns of *The Andy Griffith Show*. Certainly nothing could be wrong with enjoying Andy, Barney and Aunt Bee! Well, I would say that if it were kept within reasonable limits, watching that program would be fairly harmless. But let's be honest with ourselves. *The Andy Griffith Show* may not parade blatant sin and carnality before the viewer's eyes, but even an innocuous show like this carries a message in its programming. It is pulling the viewer into its godless storyline, thus teaching people that they don't need the Lord to have a happy, fulfilling life. Christians argue that they are not affected by all of this, but their empty claims are refuted by the way they typically live their lives.

Let's take another example: gaming. Spending a reasonable amount of time playing video games is probably not going to adversely affect a person much. However, by their very nature, video games are extremely intense. I cannot fully explain the internal process that occurs, but I do know that giving oneself over to this kind of passionate behavior has exactly the opposite effect upon one's soul as sitting in silence before the Lord. Waiting upon God tends to subdue the flesh; playing intense video games animates the flesh.

What about sports? Surely nothing could be wrong with keeping up with what is going on with one's favorite team! Well, here again, moderation is called for. Allow me to share a personal story here.

Having grown up in Northern California, I have been an Oakland Raiders fan since I was 16-years-old. Before coming to the Lord, I watched nearly every one of their games on TV and even attended a number of them at the Oakland Coliseum. Truly, this football team was an idol in my life. When I became a believer, I knew I had to walk away from this pastime. For at least ten years I paid no attention to how they were doing or even who was on the team.

Then, I began to occasionally read the game results on Mondays. I had opened the door a crack but managed to keep it limited to that for a number of years. One day, however, I noticed that there was a website that carried daily editorials about the Raiders written by Bay Area sportswriters. I started reading those articles every day. I told myself that there was no sex, violence or hidden agendas. These were simply articles about the team and its players. But what I began to notice was that my mind was continually drifting over to thinking about the team. Even in times when I would normally pray for others I found it was a lot easier and more enjoyable to daydream about the Raiders. Once I realized what was happening to me, I quit going back to that website. Consequently, the idol that I had allowed to resurface faded once more into oblivion.

The truth is that even many amusements that we would consider innocent come with a price. Born again believers are, in a very real sense, containers of the Holy Spirit. When Christians toy around with things that cater to the flesh, spiritual leakage occurs in some inexplicable way. Obviously, the more carnal a pastime is, the greater the effects will be on the person's spiritual life. But just as true is the fact that "the little foxes" (Song of Solomon 2:15) have been the ruin of many a Christian's life.

There is one more benefit to showing moderation in one's pursuit of pleasure which I will illustrate with the following scenario. Imagine two people sitting down to eat a meal that is a favorite of both. One person mildly enjoys the food, while the other savors every bite as if it were the best meal he has ever eaten. Why is there such a wide variance in their levels of enjoyment? The second person has been fasting for two days.

Allow me to return to the issue of watching television. Kathy and I have not had network, cable or satellite TV in our home for 22 years, as of this writing. We do have a television set with a DVD player. Thus, by limiting ourselves to watching DVD's, we have complete control over what we see. We don't have to be concerned about accidentally seeing some raunchy scene or hearing some blasphemous remark. We typically watch two or three videos a month: usually one G-rated movie and a couple of documentaries (e.g., National Geographic productions).

The unexpected benefit to this sparse viewing is that when we do watch something, it is extremely enjoyable! If we happen to be with people who are regular TV watchers, the difference in the level of interest is astounding. The others watch the program with mild interest, while we are utterly engrossed!

The bottom line for us is that our life with God means more to us than temporary distractions like sports, video games or television. I'm convinced that one of the main ingredients to our intimacy with God is the way we have guarded our hearts and have refused to make provision for the flesh.

HEART CHOICES

There is an important term which stands in the middle of Paul's statement ("lovers of pleasure rather than lovers of God") which would be very easy to overlook; it is the word *rather* (Gk. *mallon*).

One is immediately reminded of two occasions that Jesus used this term: "…men loved the darkness *rather* than the Light, for their deeds were evil;" (John 3:19) and "they loved the approval of men *rather* than the approval of God." (John 12:43)

Likewise, Paul says that most end-times Christians will prefer things that gratify their flesh more than, and instead of, the kinds of activities which would lead them into a close walk with God. Yes, these people have a "form of godliness." They are the first ones to say, "Lord, Lord." You will find them singing in the choir, involved in church work and listening to Christian radio. But when it comes right down to it, they despise (think little of) God, while reserving the real devotion of their hearts to what the world offers. (Matthew 6:24)

In my book, *Intoxicated with Babylon*, I stated the same principle this way:

> Make no mistake about it—there is an intense battle for the heart of every single person who professes Christ as Lord. John admonished believers, "Do not love the world, nor the things in the world. If anyone loves the world, the love of the Father is not in him." This clear-cut statement describes the fierce competition which goes on for a person's devotion, for a person's heart. At any rate, he is either devoted to God or he is not, the tell-tale factor lying in the true interests of his life. Jesus said it this way: "For where your treasure is, there will your heart be also." (Matthew 6:21) A person's treasure is simply that which is most valuable to him, what he *loves*. Without exception, a person will be led throughout life by what he cherishes most...

> When John said, "If anyone loves the world, the love of the Father is not in him," he was describing the narrow path and the broad way. Will the primary recipient of his devotion be God? Or will he selfishly devote himself to pursuing the flesh-gratifying things this world has to offer him? The devil attempts to paint gray what God paints black and white. Some may say that the believer should not love the things of this world *too*

much, but John said that we are not to love the things of this world *at all*! If someone is into what this world system offers, he simply does not love God. The Bible is quite clear concerning this...

In spite of the fact that the enemy has used sooth-saying preachers to gloss over these clear-cut statements, it cannot be any plainer: A person will either serve his lust for what the world offers, or he will serve a holy desire to please his God.[11]

Modern conveniences and sources of entertainment have allowed people to crowd an incredible amount of carnal pleasure into their lives—all of which the flesh loves! By living lifestyles that essentially make provision for and gratify the flesh, we have opened ourselves up to an increasing attraction to sin.

"What many churches are offering America is a new religion that guarantees no hell and requires no holiness. It is a limp, spineless Christianity that does not confront sin for fear of being judgmental. It is an impotent gospel that tells people everything is okay. We are more concerned with acceptance of men, than we are about pleasing God." ❧ Thomas Trask, farewell speech as General Superintendent of the Assemblies of God.[1]

"Instead of the Church being and giving a protest against the world, the world was creeping into the Church, and corrupting it. The Church grievously lowers its position when it endures sin within its [membership], and when it retains within it those who, while nominally holding the Christian faith, do not live the Christian life." ❧ C. Clemance[2]

Chapter Eleven:

CULTURE OF CORRUPTION

"They have eyes full of harlotry, insatiable for sin."
(II Peter 2:14a AMP)

"Such will be the spread of evil that many people's
love will grow cold." (Matthew 24:12 GNB)

B iblical prophets are all in agreement that the Last Days will be a time of unprecedented evil upon the earth, and even within the professing Church. In His Last Days dissertation found in Luke 17, Jesus compared that time to what it was like when Noah lived* and to the pervasive immorality of Sodom and Gomorrah.† Paul said that the Last Days would be a time when "evil men and impostors will proceed from bad to worse, deceiving and being deceived." (II Timothy 3:13) He called it perilous! (II Timothy 3:1 KJV)

But when Peter addressed the spiritual condition of the end-times, he used a couple of terms that are very interesting. They are found in the following statements he wrote: "those who indulge the flesh in its *corrupt* (Gk. *miasmos*) desires... promising them freedom while they themselves are slaves of

---

* "...the wickedness of man was great on the earth, and that every intent of the thoughts of his heart was only evil continually...all flesh had corrupted their way upon the earth." (Genesis 6:5, 12)

† "Now the men of Sodom were wicked exceedingly and sinners against the Lord." (Genesis 13:13)

corruption (Gk. *phthora*)…" (II Peter 2:10, 19)

To fully grasp the moral climate of the Last Days, it is important to understand these two Greek terms. Let's begin by looking at the first phrase from other Bible translations.

- Those who walk after the flesh and indulge in the lust of polluting passion…(AMP)
- Those who go after the unclean desires of the flesh…(BBE)
- Those who follow their filthy bodily lusts…(GNB)
- Those who are abandoned to sensuality—craving, as they do, for polluted things…(WEY)
- Those who have indulged all the foulness of their lower natures…(PHP)

Thayer's Lexicon defines *miasmos*: "that which defiles; vices the foulness of which contaminates one in his contact with the ungodly mass of mankind."[3] One can only imagine how much true believers are being spiritually polluted by those in their midst who are regularly engaging in deeds of wickedness. What is interesting about this Greek word *miasmos* is that it was later transliterated into the English language. The Webster dictionary defines this old term as: "poisonous vapor formerly supposed to arise from decomposing animal or vegetable matter, swamps, etc. and infect the air…"[4]

The Old World idea behind this term was that there were swamps that would emit noxious, poisonous vapors. If one wandered into one of these bogs, the deadly fog hovering in the area would not only hinder him from finding his way out but would slowly poison him.

What an apt picture of the spiritual atmosphere you and I live in every day. We continually breathe spiritual pollution and have become far more contaminated by it than we realize. In the eighth chapter I mentioned how the movie character

Russell Carlisle became "trapped in a wicked world to which you and I have become shamefully accustomed." How could we be surrounded by a virtual Sodom and Gomorrah and be so unconcerned about it? Because we ourselves have been terribly corrupted by it. The American Church is engulfed in a great *miasma* and cannot find her way out. Most Christians are not nearly as connected to God as they imagine.

The other Greek term Peter used is also very interesting. Thayer's Lexicon defines *phthora*: "1) corruption, destruction, perishing; 1a) that which is subject to corruption, what is perishable; 1b) in the Christian sense, eternal misery in hell; 2) in the NT, in an ethical sense, corruption, i.e. moral decay."[5] Consider how the noun and verb form of this word are used elsewhere.

- For the one who sows to his own flesh will from the flesh reap *corruption* (*phthora*)...(Galatians 6:8)
- For...you may become partakers of the divine nature, having escaped the *corruption* (*phthora*) that is in the world by lust. (II Peter 1:4)
- If any man *destroys* (*phtheiro*) the temple of God, God will destroy (*phtheiro*) him...(I Corinthians 3:17)
- Do not be deceived: "Bad company *corrupts* (*phtheiro*) good morals." (I Corinthians 15:33)
- But I am afraid that, as the serpent deceived Eve by his craftiness, your minds will be *led astray* (*phtheiro*) from the simplicity and purity of devotion to Christ. (II Corinthians 11:3)
- He has judged the great harlot who was *corrupting* (*phtheiro*) the earth with her immorality... (Revelation 19:2)

This is the corruption that permeated mankind before the great Flood. This is the moral climate that prevailed in Sodom and

Gomorrah. And this is what Paul predicted would be pervasive in the end-times Church. If I could sum up all of the verses above into one statement about the Last Days, it would be something like this: *Rather than becoming partakers of God's nature, many professing Christians will continue to serve the lusts of their flesh, corrupting their temples by subjecting themselves to worldly influences, and through it all straying from their devotion to Christ. This is the great harlot—the Apostate Church.* Dear one, I don't think I'm too far off base with this summation.

There is simply no skirting the fact that when Christians spend time sowing to the flesh‡ or indulging in sin, a deep corruption is working itself into their beings that will later come out of them through corrupt behavior of one sort or another.

Sowing and reaping is one spiritual law among many. For instance, Jesus said, "For in the way you judge, you will be judged; and by your standard of measure, it will be measured to you." (Matthew 7:2) That is a spiritual principle that cannot be avoided. Solomon offers another example: "Pride goes before destruction, and a haughty spirit before stumbling." (Proverbs 16:18) These laws of the unseen realm operate much the same as the law of gravity works in the physical realm. If a man jumps from a tall building, he will be yanked to earth by gravity. He can claim a doctrine that refutes this, but he will find that this law is immutable. By the same token, Christians can claim to love God, but if the reality of their daily lives is that they are sowing to the flesh, they *will* reap a harvest of corruption and destruction.

THE CORRUPTING NATURE OF SIN

Another sure sign of decay in the Church is when she has lost her sense of the evil nature of sin—something which has certainly happened in our day.

---

‡ It should be noted that "sowing to the flesh" can describe any carnal activity. Sin corrupts a person's being more deeply and pervasively but being involved in fleshly or worldly activities take their toll as well.

In a general way, Christians understand that man's inner life is diseased with sin. Evangelical jargon incorporates the terms "flesh" and "Self" which Scripture uses to emphasize the fallen condition of the human soul. But it remains questionable whether the malignant nature of sin is fully appreciated today.

While it is true that our nature is inherently sinful, it is also true that the more a person indulges sin, the more he will be corrupted by it. When a person gives over to some particular sinful habit, a spiritual contamination begins to work its way through his constitution. Self becomes a demanding tyrant. The overruling and unconscious question that looms within the heart becomes, "What's in it for me?" (Job 21:15) Decisions made throughout the course of any given day go through this filter. The person's gifts (intellect, wit, friendliness, leadership, memory, etc.) are used to exalt Self. One's motives, attitudes, imagination, and values all become warped by selfishness.

The more a person gives over to a sin, the more he will desire it. The contaminating effects of it ceaselessly work inside him, quietly turning his soul into something misshapen—"bent" as C.S. Lewis once said. This doesn't occur overnight but gradually. Every sin indulged in becomes one more contaminating spot of cancer upon the soul.

Little by little, the conscience is seared, thus losing its ability to operate as the moral guardian of the soul. In fact, a person cannot persist in habitual sin *without* hardening his heart. Over time, one's perspectives become altered—imperceptibly at first—but a definite change begins to take place within him. Before he is aware of what has happened to him, right is seen as wrong, wisdom as foolishness and good as evil.

J.C. Ryle captures sin's utterly deceptive nature:

> You may see this deceitfulness in the wonderful proneness of men to regard sin as less sinful and dangerous than it is in the sight of God and in

their readiness to extenuate it, make excuses for it and minimize its guilt. "It is but a little one! God is merciful!"…

Men try to cheat themselves into the belief that sin is not quite so sinful as God says it is, and that they are not so bad as they really are…We are too apt to forget that temptation to sin will rarely present itself to us in its true colors, saying, "I am your deadly enemy and I want to ruin you forever in hell." Oh, no! Sin comes to us, like Judas, with a kiss, and like Joab, with an outstretched hand and flattering words.[6]

Even though we are prone to coddle the little monster, its sole aim is to destroy its host. Indeed, left unchecked, it would gladly dethrone God Himself if given half the opportunity. Who can comprehend all the sorrow and misery sin has exacted upon mankind? If Christians could really see the effect it is having on them and on those around them, surely they would be less willing to tolerate it in their midst. Aaron Merritt Hill accurately captured the horrors of its fruit:

Suppose we could assemble, in one vast concourse of suffering, the pain-stricken, the diseased, the maimed, the lame, the halt, the blind, the distressed, the bleeding, the broken; could empty all hospitals and sick-rooms, and invalid chambers; could spread side by side all earth's convulsed death-beds; could swing the doors of its asylums and let the inmates be marshaled in one vast army of madness and driveling idiocy; could bring the anguished babes, the famine-pinched, the bereaved mothers, and all the bowed and wrinkled and infirm children of age; could unlock our dungeons and empty all our scaffolds, bring all suffering criminals and inebriates, the weary, the heartbroken, the passion-tossed—bring every one from every quarter of the earth who has an ache or a burden or an infirmity or a disease or a wound occasioned by sin, to this common assemblage of woe! Great God! who but thee could bear the unutterable vision? What finite ear could endure the cries and groans and maniac shrieks and sobs and sighs and wails of this hideous, frightful chorus of physical woes which sin ever occasions?[7]

CORRUPTION IN THE CHURCH

I believe there are two primary reasons that the Church is undergoing moral decay today. First, most Christians are regularly immersing themselves in the world's degenerate value system by watching television, listening to secular radio, surfing the Internet and living for the world's prizes. I have already discussed at length how the spirit of the world has successfully cast its spell upon the minds and hearts of Christians.

The second factor involved in this process of corruption is that people are no longer dealing with the sin in their lives. I intend to deal with this subject more fully in later chapters, but I touch on it here because it is having such a huge effect upon the spiritual health of the Body of Christ as a whole.

One aspect I will mention here briefly is the fact that multiple thousands of Christians are regularly viewing pornography. I wrote about the effects of this in my book, *How America Lost Her Innocence*:

> How is this affecting the Body of Christ? When Jesus warned us to "beware of the leaven of hypocrisy," He was communicating to His listeners that even though a hypocrite hides his sin from those around him, it still has a detrimental effect on the lives of others. The metaphor of leaven is used to illustrate the corrupting

influence of a small ingredient upon the rest of the dough. Unfortunately, in the case of the 21st Century Church, we are talking about the influence of millions of men who are outwardly presenting themselves as religious while inwardly maintaining a virtual mental library of pornographic images.

Despite the soothsayers who minimize the damage being done, pornography is a spiritual disease running rampant through the Christian community. In short, we show all the signs of suffering from a spiritual epidemic.

If it is true that one out of every five men sitting in America's pews is saturating his mind with the evil images of pornography, how does this affect the overall level of godliness in the Church? The answer is devastatingly obvious: The general urgency to live a consecrated life is now at an all-time low. Self-centered living has all but replaced true sacrificial love. A hunger for God has been supplanted by a lust for entertainment. While the Church is weathering a fierce spiritual onslaught from without, the godly character needed for this battle rots within.[8]

Yes, just when the Body of Christ needs on-fire saints to call us back to holy living, we find that a cold formalism is quickly setting up within us. Just like the First Century Jewish leaders, we have traded a passionate love of God for the outward semblance of religion.

"A hypocrite is [harder to convert] than a gross sinner; the form of godliness, if that be rested in, becomes one of Satan's strongholds, by which he opposes the power of godliness."
~ Matthew Henry[1]

"He that boasts of being one of God's elect, while he is willfully and habitually living in sin, is only deceiving himself, and talking wicked blasphemy. Of course, it is hard to know what people really are and many, who make a fair show outwardly in religion, may turn out at last to be rotten-hearted hypocrites." ~ J.C. Ryle[2]

"A religion of mere emotion and sensationalism is the most terrible of all curses that can come upon any people. The absence of reality is sad enough, but the aggravation of pretence is a deadly sin." ~ Samuel Chadwick[3]

Chapter Twelve:

A FORM OF GODLINESS

"They will maintain a façade of 'religion,'
but their conduct will deny its validity."
(II Timothy 3:5 PHP)

A s Paul was laying out his description of the Church at the end of the age, he saw that there would be many with nothing more than "a form of godliness." (II Timothy 3:5) In its barest sense, this must mean these people would have the outward trappings of a walk with God but lack the inward reality. One of the terrifying realities of Christianity is that it is possible for people to live with an outward semblance of faith while, at the same time, they are resisting the inward work of the Holy Spirit.

People with a form of godliness have opted for a Christian existence where they convey to others that they have a viable spiritual life which they don't really possess. They have exaggerated their spirituality for so long that they have actually come to believe the lie.

Just as Self and pride can manifest themselves in a thousand ways within different people, so too can false piety. For the sake of identifying this phenomenon more clearly, I will touch on three of the most common "forms of godliness" that I see at work in people's lives.

Outward Appearances

If there was one thing the Apostle Paul knew from intimate experience, it was hypocrisy. He had lived in it for so long that he could "smell it a mile away." He detested it because he knew how it had kept him locked in a prison of Self and hopelessly distant from God.

He had been a Pharisee, and, as such, had been far more concerned about how he appeared to others than God. Jesus borrowed the Greek word *hypocrite*—used in the Greek world to describe actors assuming a stage role—as the most fitting term available to describe the false piety of the Pharisees. "They loved the approval of men rather than the approval of God." (John 12:43)

The postmodern Church has developed its own kind of hypocrisy—tailor-made for today's American lifestyle. Although our evangelical churches don't have ministers parading around with phylacteries and long tassels hanging off their clothes, we have created our own brand of Phariseeism. Like the Pharisees, many people have become professional religious actors who are spiritually empty inside. They go to church because it is the right thing to do. They mimic what they see in the lives of others. They present an outward image of what they think others want to see in them. Indeed, it is much easier to exaggerate one's godliness than to fight for the real thing.

A person who is immersed in worldly activities should not act as though he is living a consecrated life. A churchgoer who overeats or masturbates or indulges in other carnal activities should not promote an image of godliness to those around him. Someone who is out of control with spending (e.g., running up credit cards, buying unnecessary luxuries, etc.) should not present himself as a committed believer. One who has no inclination to regularly spend time in God's Word or lacks the commitment to living out biblical precepts should not volunteer to teach classes or mentor others in the church. These are only a few examples of ways modern Christians exaggerate their level of godliness to other people. But the reality is that anyone whose inner world is out of alignment with the outer image they project to others is settling for a "form of godliness."

Jesus warned His disciples about the contamination of false spirituality: "Beware of the leaven of the Pharisees, which is hypocrisy." (Luke 12:1) The best analogy in our day and age to this admonition would be the warnings one might encounter along a highway: "CAUTION! WARNING! STOP! DANGER! WATCH OUT!" For Jesus to use such a strong term as "beware" shows how extremely hazardous He considered hypocrisy to be. The following are some of the reasons it is so dangerous:

- It reinforces a person's Self-love;
- It is hard to detect;
- It substitutes a false spirituality for the real thing;
- It breeds further deception and delusion;
- It hinders a person from seeing his need to change and repent;
- It fosters fear of man rather than fear of God;
- It magnifies the immediate dividends while blinding one to the eternal consequences.

It should be noted that a man's true spiritual condition is not determined by an optimistic self-evaluation. He is not godly simply because he considers himself to be. Nor is he devout because he has fooled others into thinking he is. The reality of his spiritual condition is based upon one thing only: how God sees him. The writer of Hebrews said, "And there is no creature hidden from His sight, but all things are open and laid bare to the eyes of Him with whom we have to do." (Hebrews 4:13) Those who are bitter, unforgiving, lustful, greedy, envious, critical of others or full of self-pity are seen for what they really are by the

Lord. They may convince themselves and others that they truly walk with the Lord, but that doesn't necessarily make it so.

DE-EMPHASIZING VITAL TRUTH

Another way that a person can opt for "a form of godliness" rather than the real thing is to focus his attention upon things of secondary importance. Jesus summarized the true foundation of religion when He quoted the following passage out of the Torah: "'You shall love the Lord your God with all your heart, and with all your soul, and with all your mind.' This is the great and foremost commandment. The second is like it, 'You shall love your neighbor as yourself.' On these two commandments depend the whole Law and the Prophets." (Matthew 22:37-40)

Any sincere believer—before or after Calvary—who has conscientiously endeavored to honestly keep these rules of life has come to know that they truly are "the great and foremost commandment(s)." He understands that "The one who does not love does not know God, for God is love." (I John 4:8) Therefore, his life is taken up with a deep devotion to the Almighty and is heavily involved with helping needy people, in one way or another.

Although I'm sure the self-deceived Pharisees thought they actually did love God and others, the truth was that they lived for Self. Love for God always translates into the daily life as devotion to others—meeting their needs. (I John 4:20) Since these Jewish religious leaders refused to sacrificially give of themselves, they simply avoided the reality of these laws by emphasizing strict adherence to secondary rules. They stressed minor points of the law and de-emphasized the heart-reality of the two greatest commandments. Consequently, over the years, they quietly changed the worship of Jehovah into dead ritualism.

One such example was the way they would carefully weigh out their fragments of spice and scrupulously extract a tenth of it to put in the offering. Jesus rebuked them by saying, "Woe to you, scribes and Pharisees, hypocrites! For you tithe mint and dill and cummin, and have neglected the weightier provisions of the law: justice and mercy and faithfulness; but these are the things you should have done without neglecting the others. You blind guides, who strain out a gnat and swallow a camel!" (Matthew 23:23-24)

Modern-day Pharisees don't meticulously weigh out spices, but they still cleverly sidestep the fundamentals of Christianity: loving God and others. An example of this nowadays is the way some overemphasize the importance of their pet doctrines, as if they constitute the paramount issue of the Christian faith. Much of the disunity and prideful contention alive within 21st Century Christendom is a direct result of those who argue and debate about doctrinal issues with anyone who holds opposing views.

Of course, it is proper to contend earnestly for the *tenets of the faith* (i.e., the virgin birth of Christ, the Trinity, etc.). However, prideful, immature people cannot tolerate differing viewpoints on secondary doctrinal issues like eternal security, women preachers, the timing of the rapture, divorce and remarriage, and so on. It is all a smokescreen for these people. By constantly stressing their favorite doctrines and de-emphasizing the things that Jesus stressed, they are able to avoid the truth about their unwillingness to live out the love of God to other people.

Jesus made it abundantly clear that the central theme of Christianity is love for the brethren. For instance, in His parting comments to the disciples before entering the Garden of Gethsemane, seven different times Jesus told them to love one another. (John 13:34, 35; 15:9, 10, 12, 17; 17:26) This theme was only strengthened by Paul, Peter and John. All of these apostles stressed the importance of meeting the needs of others. If there is one obvious truth in the New Testament about the Christian faith it is that love should be the predominant characteristic of God's people.

Surely any honest person is aware of the great need that exists around him. There are outreaches to street people that need volunteers to help. Jails and prisons abound that are brimming with lost souls who would welcome a visit or even a letter from someone who cares. Convalescent hospitals house a multitude of lonely souls about to plunge into eternal damnation. Any believer could easily spend the rest of his life involving himself in the great need surrounding him.

The interesting thing is that the very people who tend to be the most vocal about their theological opinions and quick to impose their views on others are usually the ones who are the least willing to lift a finger to get involved with others. How are they any different from the Pharisees who lived during the First Century? (Matthew 23:2-4) Their Christianity is not for God; it is all for Self.

One story that truly illustrates the tragic consequences that can come from allowing secondary doctrines to supersede more important spiritual matters is that of a man who went through the Pure Life Ministries residential program for sexual addicts. Ted was married with children but was terribly addicted to pornography when he came to PLM. However, his life underwent such a dramatic transformation during his time there that, a year after he returned home, he was asked to head up a new outreach of the ministry to other alumni.

At first things went well, but over time he left his first love. Little by little the vibrant faith he had come into at Pure Life was supplanted by the dead religion he had lived in for many years. His concern over the doctrinal positions that he had held dear while in ongoing sin began to reemerge. Finally, religion won out in his heart and he informed me that he felt he had to disassociate himself from us. I was very concerned about the spiritual direction he was going and pleaded with him to reconsider his decision. My letter to him went unheeded, but eighteen months later I received the following letter from him:

> I write this letter to express my deep regret over my decision to separate from PLM—a ministry and a

people that have helped me in ways I can't even begin to put into words. I humbly request your forgiveness and that of the entire PLM staff, whom I fear my actions have also offended.

The pride which motivated me to part from PLM was just the beginning of a slippery slide back into sin. At the time, I felt that my "doctrinal reasons" for parting from the ministry were correct and I am afraid that I took great pride in that. I was wrong. Your compassionate warnings to me went unheeded and so the pride coupled with ceasing to be involved in the lives of others, getting wrapped up in the small package of self and no longer seeking the Lord with my whole heart all led me down the path to spiritual destruction.

I was fired from my job last October for viewing pornography on the company computer. [My wife] asked me to leave our home and divorce is inevitable.

I can honestly say that my six months at PLM and the year that followed once I returned home were the happiest, most peace-filled months of my entire life. For the first time ever, I had an intimate walk with the Lord that was so sweet and was yielding victory over temptation and sin. PLM gave me the tools necessary to sustain that close relationship with God. But because I stopped regularly putting into practice what God gave me there, little by little I slipped back into the world and the flesh, and started believing the lies of the devil and not living in the light of God's truth.

The past year and a half has been very spiritually dark for me...In closing, please allow me to express again my sorrow over my prideful and selfish actions. My heart's desire is that the fellowship once shared with all of you can be restored.

Ted's story is a perfect illustration of what can happen to someone who becomes more concerned about doctrinal viewpoints than the fundamental issue of Christianity: love for God and others.

BUILDING FAITH ON FEELINGS

Perhaps the largest group of people who hold to a "form of godliness" in lieu of true Christianity are those who substitute faith with feelings. American culture has deified our feelings with such maxims as, "If I feel it, it must be right." Psychology has become the study of emotions much more than the study of mental processes. Millions of people are turning to mood-altering prescription drugs in search of euphoria and tranquility. It is not surprising then that many would bring this same mindset into the Church and attempt to build their faith on the faulty foundation of feelings. Perhaps some examples will clarify what is happening in many of our churches.

Brenda is very involved in the women's ministry of her upscale, suburban church. She seems to come alive when she connects with other women. She regularly gets involved in long telephone calls with other ladies, where the two will recount in great detail all of the "spiritual" experiences they have enjoyed lately. At the weekly women's meeting, she typically can be found praying her heart out over one of the other women, weeping as she "intercedes." Her emotional displays are also extended into her highly subjective relationship with God where she imagines that her constant bouts of weeping are a sure sign of God's touching her.

Meanwhile, back at home her relationship with her husband is very strained because she is so emotionally demanding of him. She brought an unrealistic, romantic expectation into the marriage that she and her Prince Charming would spend the rest of their lives together sharing deeply emotional experiences.

She grew resentful when he proved to be a little more down-to-earth than that. Her underlying resentment often boils up in ugly outbursts. Her treatment of her husband is clear proof that her "spiritual" encounters have not been with the Lord.

Women aren't the only ones in the Church who base their Christianity upon their feelings. Jim is a reticent, quiet man who worked for a number of years at a Christian rehabilitation center. Over time he became increasingly concerned about the lack of true spirituality in the ministry.

> The chapel services became the focal point of the program, with raucous, hand-clapping music and loud, emotionally-driven preaching. The most appreciated speakers were those who could deliver a rousing message full of flattery and emotional appeals—all of which was designed to make the men feel good about themselves. These cheer-leading sermons often ended in altar calls which promised a special touch or blessing from the Lord.
>
> In a center ministering to men given over to ongoing sin, repentance was a message rarely heard. Rather than maturely pastoring these men into steady spiritual progress by emphasizing the importance of daily obedience, self-discipline and a solid devotional life, they were taught to look to the exuberance of their chapel services as their main source of spiritual sustenance. Little wonder then that there was such a high percentage of men who returned back to the feelings-oriented lifestyle of drug addiction.

This style of spiritual leadership can be found in many churches as well. It should go without saying that the decimal level of a church service does not determine the level of God's presence in the place. A loud church can be just as dead or alive as a quiet one and vice-versa.

The last example of replacing faith with feelings is in the realm of worship. This is a tricky subject to tackle because emotions do play a part in worship. Connecting with the Lord through the expression of one's adoration of Him can be a powerful and moving experience. "Such people the Father seeks to be His worshipers." (John 4:23) A sincere expression of love from an obedient son or daughter is certainly one of the greatest joys the Father can have. It could even be considered the pinnacle of our interaction with Him.

So what could be wrong with raising one's voice together with a host of other believers in praise to the Lord? Absolutely nothing if it is done "in spirit and truth." (John 4:24) Problems in worship arise when people sing "in the flesh and insincerity."

Casual Christians blithely mouthing the words of hymns (songs that contain rich, profound expressions of love for God that they have no comprehension of and whom they pay little attention to) is not worship.

Just as repulsive to Him are those who love worship for what they can get out of it for Self; meaning, they do not worship out of a love for God but because they enjoy the emotional "high" they experience through the music. The danger of losing oneself in the thrills that can accompany powerful worship times is that the person is not focused upon God but upon what he or she is feeling. If Self rather than God is at the center of the experience, it's not true worship.

I've attempted to present my honest concerns over the preeminence feelings are often given in the Church. Obviously, there is a place for Christian women to express and share their emotions with each other; there is nothing wrong with uplifting sermons that encourage the saints; worship services that lead believers into a sense of spiritual exhilaration can be marvelous.

All of these things are good IF they do not take the place of a submissive relationship with God. Believers who attempt to live by their fluctuating feelings are headed for disaster. Faith is living above the realm of our feelings. True faith in Christ holds steady through the inevitable ebbs and flows of life.

It is difficult to ascertain exactly what went through Paul's mind when he wrote about Last Days Christians who were content with "a form of godliness." It seems evident to me that as his mind became filled with thoughts of the Church at the end of the age that he envisioned a majority of churchgoers who would be content with a mere semblance of Christianity. The people he saw in his mind's eye would prefer to convey an image to those around them that they were walking with the Lord—although it really wasn't so. No matter how their particular "form of godliness" took shape, one common denominator among them all was that they would be unwilling to allow the Holy Spirit to expose the reality of what was in their hearts. These people would live an outward expression of Christianity while resisting the power that came from a God who desired to do a deep, inward work in their hearts.

"Let us be very sure that we do not substitute church membership, coming to church or chapel, going to prayer-meeting, teaching in Sunday-schools, reading devout books, and the like, for inward submission to the power."
🙨 Alexander MacLaren[1]

"O God, give us more men aflame for Thee!—men...with burning hearts, brimming eyes, and bursting lips; men who fear nothing but sin, love nothing but Thy supreme will, desire nothing but to die that other men might live. Holy Father, I ask Thee in Jesus' Name to give us these men, lest the Church continue to drift farther and farther from the norm as revealed in The Acts..." 🙨 Leonard Ravenhill[2]

*"They will act religious, but they will reject
the power that could make them godly.
Stay away from people like that!"*
(II Timothy 3:5 NLT)

In 2,000 years of history, the gospel has never seen the
level of success it is enjoying today in America. There have
never been so many conversions, so many churches and so
much money to support the evangelical enterprise. Christianity
permeates every facet of American life. We have Christian
recording artists, Christian baseball stars, Christian politicians,
Christian millionaires and even a Christian heavyweight champ!
Everywhere we turn in the field of ministry, we find bank
accounts bulging, numbers increasing, organizations expanding
and denominations flourishing. Surely, the gospel has never
seen such outstanding results! Yet, with all the progress and
outward signs of success, why is there such little power in the
lives of believers?

Yes, we live in a nation that has been thoroughly
Christianized, but how many "Christians" are truly believers? I
suspect that there is a vast difference between the gospel Paul
preached and that which we see permeating the airwaves today.
The Apostle Paul described the gospel as "the power of God…"

(Romans 1:16) It is not dogma. It is not a social movement called Evangelicalism. It is not found in the academic dissertations of some lifeless seminary. The gospel—whether or not we want to acknowledge this—is simply the power of God at work in the lives of people. If you see the power of God working, you will see the gospel being enacted before your eyes. If you don't see this divine energy at work in people's lives, then what you are witnessing is either an anemic replica or an outright fraud.

I believe there is a longing in the hearts of true believers to experience God's power. They want to see something real from the Lord; they are tired of carnal messages that cater to their emotions or academic sermons aimed at their intellects. They want to hear a fresh word from the Lord. They long to be touched in the heart by words that have the unction of the Holy Spirit. They want to sense divine energy moving inside them, invigorating them, empowering them, kindling a new love for Jesus.

Scripture promises this kind of life experience to Christians—and it wasn't meant only for those who lived in a different era. God's power is available for us today!

The epic story of the Old Testament points to the irrefutable fact that man is weak and is dependent upon a power that lies outside of him. It is a long history lesson that tells about God's supernatural work among man. With the strength of His right hand He destroyed mankind with a flood, rained fire from heaven upon Sodom and Gomorrah, decimated the nation of Egypt with plagues, and destroyed 185,000 Assyrian soldiers in one night. The Lord used His might to protect and bless His people.

In the New Testament period, the Son of God came exhibiting a more subtle form of this divine force. The primary difference in the way God interacted with His people was that He worked on their behalf in more of an outward way during the O.T. period; since Calvary, that power has been directed more toward the inward life of His children.

There is a mighty force from heaven that is available to every child of God. The Lord greatly desires for His children to be "clothed with power from on high." (Luke 24:49) He wants them to know about "the surpassing greatness of His power toward us who believe." (Ephesians 1:18-19) He wants it to be real that He "has not given us a spirit of timidity, but of power and love and discipline." (II Timothy 1:7) He longs for believers to taste "the powers of the age to come," (Hebrews 6:5) and to experience "the power of an indestructible life." (Hebrews 7:16) He wants them to be "strengthened with all power, according to His glorious might…" (Colossians 1:11) This kind of power is seen in the lives of true saints.

TRANSFORMING POWER

One of the primary functions of God's power is the transformation of sinners into saints. It is a process the New Testament calls sanctification, whereby the common or unclean is made holy. The work of regeneration that begins with rebirth is only the beginning of God's work in the human soul. It is going through the "narrow gate" of repentance which allows the person to begin his lifelong journey on the "narrow way." True Christianity offers the sincere adherent a life that is becoming increasingly free from the poisonous touch of sin.

The truth is that even the most "together" believer must conquer stubborn, sinful habit patterns, overcome a demanding flesh, deal with a selfish nature and subdue an ever-surging pride. He must face all of this, while at the same time, living in a world system that entices him to sin and mocks true Christianity. As if that were not enough to overwhelm the most stout-hearted person, he also is forced to deal with a relentless, determined foe who is bent upon his destruction. The poor man looks within himself for the strength to undertake this great battle and all he finds is spiritual inertia and a lack of resolve. Is there any hope for him? Can he ever be holy?

With marvelous audacity Christianity steps forward and claims to have the wherewithal to bring about change in the worst of characters. What, but the power of God, can flush the filth out of the heart of a sexual addict and leave innocence and purity in its wake? What else but the Indwelling Spirit can change a hopeless drunk or drug addict into a sober-minded man? Who else but God can transform a thief into a man of virtue, a liar into a lover of truth, a mocker into a serious-minded man or an arrogant braggart into a meek lamb? Only God can work such human miracles—but He does do it!

The great need for Christians today is for the invigorating life of God to flow through their beings, enlightening their minds with spiritual truth, purifying their motives, fortifying their convictions, molding their personalities, solidifying their vacillating wills, sweetening their natures, cleansing and renewing their hearts and subduing their flesh. We need to be revitalized and energized by the quickening power of the Holy Spirit.

Can God do this? My testimony is that I have seen it happen countless times in the most hopeless situations. Let the skeptics—both outside and within the Church—line up with their sneering cynicism and faithless denials of God's power. If they could but see within the walls of the celestial city, a hundred million saints would step forth with resounding testimonies to the fact that the Almighty converted them from virtual devils into loving saints.

For two millennia Christ has been transforming people from the inside out. He can, and still does, perform this great work within people's souls today. The power of God is available for those who will claim it by faith. "I can do all things through Christ who strengthens me." (Philippians 4:13)

POWER OUTAGE

God's quiet power working within people has been the hallmark of true believers from the very beginning. However, as the Lord opened the Apostle Paul's heart to see the Church during the final days of man, something quite different— something deformed and misshapen—emerged in his mind's eye. The vast majority of professing Christians he saw were actually doing their utmost to resist that power, preferring what was little more than an outward semblance of Christianity. These people were "holding to a form of godliness, although they have denied its power..." (II Timothy 3:5) The Good News Bible paraphrases this verse as: "They will hold to the outward form of our religion, but reject its real power." I believe this is what we are witnessing in much of the Church today.

There can be little question as to what the venerable apostle meant by this statement. He was describing a kind of religion where God is kept at bay; where His efforts to sanctify and purify the person are hindered. The people being described are resisting the convicting work of the Holy Spirit. Rather than submitting themselves to the lordship of Christ, they have taken Christianity on their own terms. They have remained lord of their own lives; Self has retained its position of authority in their hearts. Without the efficacious work of the Holy Ghost in a person's life, what is left but "a form of godliness?"

As we have already seen, there have always been hypocrites attached to the true Church. In every age there have been those who have settled for the outward appearance of holiness but have been unwilling to allow God to really deal with them inside. There have always been hearers of the word who had no sincere willingness to live what they were being taught.

Indeed, any sincere believer will attest to the fact that he has gone through periods where his life with God has become stale. It is simply an unfortunate aspect of the human heart that it will occasionally drift away from the Lord. There seems to be a hardening agent in the heart that causes it to become rigid. Just as cement trucks must constantly churn the concrete within them, believers periodically need a fresh breeze from heaven to pull them out of stagnation. This is a normal part of the Christian life. However, when Paul talked about those with "a form of godliness," he wasn't describing occasional periods of spiritual dryness but hypocrisy on an enormous scale.

DENYING THE POWER

The question that arises out of this is how the Church has come to the point that hypocrisy has overtaken holiness as one of its prevailing features. I believe that a number of trends have emerged that have ushered in this spiritual malnourishment which is now so commonplace.

The first influencing factor I will mention is the teaching that overemphasizes grace to the point where people disconnect their spiritual condition from their behavior, adopting the mindset that what they do in their daily lives doesn't really matter. Jude foretold that during the end-times there would be those who "turn the grace of our God into licentiousness." (Jude 1:4) This mindset has so gripped Christendom that multitudes of men regularly view and participate in the most vile behavior and believe they are in good standing with God.

This falsehood has lodged itself in the Church the same way that most heresies do. When men stress the importance of one aspect of Christianity at the expense of others, false teaching is certain to come forth. I wrote about this in my book *Intoxicated with Babylon*:

Entire denominations and church movements teach that a person does not really have to obey God. This false message is loudly proclaimed from pulpits, over Christian radio, and through a barrage of books aimed at giving churchgoers a false sense of security. Its vocal proponents shout down anyone who counters it. "You're teaching legalism! You're telling people they have to earn their way to heaven! There is nothing a person can do to save himself. It's all God's grace!"

As with most deceptions there is usually enough truth embedded in the message to make it believable. And it should be acknowledged that a strongly legalistic presentation of Christianity lends itself to a "saved by works" understanding of the Gospel. But there isn't enough of that unbalanced teaching in church circles to warrant the overwhelming emphasis on grace that Christendom has heard in the last 10-20 years. One would think that legalism is the greatest threat the Church has ever faced, considering the inundation of teachings given on grace. The truth of the matter is that the real threat is from those teachings which have, in the name of Grace, encouraged believers to indulge themselves in a selfish and worldly lifestyle, far from the abundant life Jesus had in mind for His Bride.[3]

Another phenomenon that has grown over the years is what I would term *osmosis listening*. This is the unspoken attitude held by many that they will grow godlier simply by reading Christian books and hearing inspiring sermons. Paul predicted that many members of the end-times Church would be "always learning and never able to come to the knowledge of the truth." (II Timothy 3:7) In other words, these people regularly acquire information about spiritual things, but never come into spiritual reality. They believe that they are maturing in the faith simply because they have learned more and more about spiritual matters.

The truth is that Christians don't grow spiritually through the process of academic learning. They only mature as they actually live what they are learning. Christianity is not a spectator sport where the person watches safely from the sidelines. A person isn't a believer just because he reads about Christianity any more than a fan is a football player just because he regularly attends the games of his favorite team. Christianity that isn't actually lived is not Christianity.

It is one thing for a baby believer to spiritually crawl around on "all fours" for the first two or three years of his new life. But being unable to walk years after entering the Christian faith is a sure sign that the person never experienced the new birth. He is still back at the narrow gate of decision where the prospect of following Christ is mere speculation. He entered the Gate with his mind but left his heart outside. His faith is nothing more than mental activity.

The last factor in this corporate loss of God's power is simply the effect of thirty-plus years of turning to the worldly answers psychology has provided for defining and treating people's personal problems. Placing heavy stress on the quality of a person's upbringing has enabled many to conclude that their sinful behavior is merely the direct result of past victimization. This belief system has so overtaken the Church that even people in the most blatant forms of sin are now convinced of their own innocence because in some way or another they have been victimized by others. This unwillingness to accept personal responsibility for their actions causes them to bypass the repentance that will bring them into true freedom.

It should go without saying that it is natural for fallen man to avoid taking responsibility for sinful behavior. Adam and Eve's response in the Garden to God's interrogation is proof of this truth. No sooner had sin entered their beings than they were already attempting to minimize and explain it away. Accordingly, most of the teachings of psychology are designed to help people who are content with a "form of godliness" and are unwilling to allow God to deal with their un-Christlike attitudes and behaviors.

Godliness is no longer the goal; now the primary objective is to make people feel better. Rather than approaching God in contrition, looking for His power to transform their hearts, they have been taught to go to the "professional" who can help them to understand themselves and why they struggle. Nevertheless, the truth remains that the power of the Holy Spirit is available to anyone who will humble himself in repentance and allow the Lord to change his inner being.

All of these subtle teachings and attitudes have worked hand-in-hand to create a national mindset within the American Church. A licentious presentation of Grace offers a form of Christianity without the beauty of holiness. An academic approach to faith offers a form of Christianity that expects no change. A psychological message offers a form of Christianity without repentance. Interweave these falsehoods together into a "group think" and you end up with a powerless form of Christianity that cannot penetrate hearts.

Most evangelicals have come into this system and do not realize that it has only come about in the past 30-40 years. They have entered this anemic religious lifestyle and do not understand that this is not the real thing. They have never come under the tremendous conviction of the Holy Spirit that leaves a person frantically searching for a way to unload the dreadful weight of sin. They haven't experienced the overwhelming sensation of being forcefully corrected by the Almighty because they have treated His holiness with a flippant attitude. They don't know what it is like to emerge from hours of communion with God, hearts ablaze with a holy passion for souls.

They are content with their weak "form of godliness" because it allows them to maintain control over their own lives and worship the idols which abound in our pagan culture and which hold the true devotion of their hearts. Their god is impotent and they are happy to have him so. He is NOT the Jehovah of the Bible.

This corporate mentality has become so embedded in the Evangelical Movement that one might wonder if the entire system will have to be overthrown before real Christianity will be free to emerge.

However, we are in the Last Days and all that is occurring around us is exactly as it was foretold. As the End draws nearer, people will grow harder toward the things of God and increasingly more open to the soothing voices of false teachers telling them what they want to hear. The ongoing process of replacing Truth with falsehood will continue until professing Christians will no longer be able to discern good from evil. Surely these are perilous times!

"Weak men may be content to echo the popular cries of the day. It is too often the mission of the servant of God to contradict these familiar voices."
∽ W.F. Adeney[1]

"Jesus hath many lovers of His heavenly kingdom, but few bearers of His Cross."
∽ Thomas À Kempis[2]

"How terrible is this!—when the ambassadors of God turn agents for the devil!—when they who are commissioned to teach men the way to heaven do in fact teach them the way to hell...Those, of whatever denomination, who encourage the proud, the trifler, the passionate, the lover of the world, the man of pleasure, the unjust or unkind, the easy, careless...to imagine he is in the way to heaven. These are false prophets in the highest sense of the word. These are traitors both to God and man...They are continually peopling the realms of the night; and whenever they follow the poor souls they have destroyed, 'hell shall be moved from beneath to meet them at their coming!'" ∽ John Wesley[3]

Chapter Fourteen:

CROSSLESS CHRISTIANITY

*"For the time is coming when [people] will not
tolerate (endure) sound and wholesome instruction, but,
having ears itching [for something pleasing and gratifying],
they will gather to themselves one teacher after another to
a considerable number, chosen to satisfy their own liking
and to foster the errors they hold, and will turn aside from
hearing the truth and wander off into myths and
man-made fictions." (II Timothy 4:3-4 AMP)*

They have winsome personalities. Their message is positive—even encouraging. Thousands throng into their sanctuaries every weekend. Their doctrinal beliefs are orthodox—at least on paper. What's more, multitudes of "unchurched" lost souls are attending services and hearing the gospel preached every week. The "seeker-friendly" model of reaching unbelievers has been extremely effective.

Their success has come in large part through adherence to certain marketing strategies found in the business world. One of the key principles that governs the "seeker-sensitive" movement is that pastors should tailor their message to what their congregations want to hear. One such pastor even polled his people to find out what they were looking for in a church. Os Guiness recently expressed his concerns about these tactics.

When mega-church pastors seek to mold a message to their "market" of constituent needs, their preaching omits key components. Gone are the hard sayings of

Jesus. Gone is the teaching on sin, self-denial, sacrifice, suffering, judgment, hell. With all its need-meeting emphases, there is little in the church-growth movement that stands crosswise to the world.[4]

One of the common denominators found operating among all "seeker-sensitive" pastors is their focus upon the positive aspects of God and Christianity. To put it in modern colloquialism: "You win more flies with honey than vinegar."

Christian marketing experts have discovered that unsaved people are drawn to a message that emphasizes the love of God and de-emphasizes His judgment. The truth is that people simply don't want to hear confrontive preaching. What they *will* follow is a Christian model that is "positive and uncondemning" and doesn't make demands. But how does that line up with Scripture or the model of the early Church?

The New Testament opens with the story of John the Baptist, who brought an unequivocal message of repentance. He told the religious leaders of his day: "You brood of vipers, who warned you to flee from the wrath to come? Therefore bear fruit in keeping with repentance." (Matthew 3:7-8) He didn't exactly charm people into the faith!

When Peter gave his Holy Spirit-empowered message to the Jews on the Day of Pentecost, he accused them of murdering the Messiah. Luke wrote that "they were pierced to the heart." (Acts 2:37) When they asked him what they should do, he told them to repent. Three thousand people were saved that day!

The gospel presentation offered by those in the "seeker-friendly" movement may enjoy the same numerical successes, but notice the difference in what is presented by the following "prayer of salvation" offered by one of their well-known authors.

Do you have a relationship with Jesus Christ? If you aren't sure of this, I'd like the privilege of leading you in a prayer to settle the issue. Let's bow our heads. I'm going to pray a prayer and you can follow it silently in your mind:

'Dear God, I want to know Your purpose for my life. I don't want to waste the rest of my life on the wrong things. Today I want to take the first step in preparing for eternity by getting to know You. Jesus Christ, I don't understand it all, but as much as I know how, I want to open my life to You. I ask you to come into my life and make yourself real to me. Use this series to help me know what You made me for. Thank you. Amen.'

If you just prayed that prayer for the very first time, I congratulate you. You've just become a part of the family of God.[5]

Huh? While this may sound appealing on the surface, where is the gut-wrenching examination of their hearts and lives? (II Corinthians 13:5) Where is the acknowledgement of sin and rebellion? (II Samuel 12:13) Where is "the sorrow that is according to the will of God [which] produces a repentance without regret, leading to salvation…"? (II Corinthians 7:10) Where is the true repentance that dethrones Self as the master of the person's life and bows in submission to the lordship of Christ? (Luke 9:23-24) Where is the commitment to follow Christ wherever He leads, to do whatever He commands, to obey His will at any cost? (Luke 14:26-27) Isn't this a clear-cut example of what the Lord said during Jeremiah's time? "They have healed the brokenness of My people superficially, saying, 'Peace, peace,' but there is no peace." (Jeremiah 6:14)

Multitudes may be flocking around these teachers, but they are not entering the kingdom of God. They are simply propagating the lie that a person can be saved without really repenting of sin and renouncing his life of self-will.

While "seeker-sensitive" preachers have learned to cover their bases by telling people that they need to repent of sin, their concept of the nature of sin is so weak and generalized that anyone could say such a prayer without the slightest bit of remorse of wrongdoing. Thus, there is no real repentance taking place, and subsequently, no forgiveness. In his book, *The Jesus Sensitive Church*, Ron Auch writes the following:

> For the past few years, the Christian community has been excited about discovering a paradigm shift. In other words, we believe the old "way" of presenting the gospel is outdated and we must adapt the new "way." There has been a shift in what is accepted today. It would seem that the old way of calling sin "sin," is outdated and not very relevant. Today, we must be "spiritually correct" because the world is no longer accepting the old fashioned "hell-fire" type preaching. When was the last time you heard your pastor actually say that God considers a certain activity "sinful?"
>
> Much of what the Church is calling a "seeker-friendly service" should probably be called "sinner-friendly." Sinners can sit in their churches week after week and not realize they are in sin, but at least they feel welcomed.
>
> Some would say, "Ron, you are stuck in a rut. What you are suggesting just doesn't work anymore. Churches that preach hard against sin are not growing." This is where our pragmatism is getting in the way. We have convinced ourselves that "success" (i.e., church growth) is the ultimate goal.[6]

There is truth in the common maxim: "It's hard to argue with success." It becomes very difficult to convince the pastor of a thriving, growing church that he is actually failing in God's eyes.* But the kingdom of God operates under different principles of success; i.e. the narrow way.

When the leaders of the church growth movement assess how they are doing, they don't examine whether or not they are holding true to what the Bible really teaches about such matters; they think with a big business mentality. They gauge everything by outward, worldly perspectives. They are not concerned about people truly being transformed into the kind of disciples Jesus sought. They are looking for quantity, not quality. After taking a pulse of the Church recently, Christian pollster George Barna wrote:

> The most discouraging study we ever conducted was one in which we attempted to identify churches in the U.S. that consistently and intelligently evaluate life transformation among the people to whom they minister. We found that very few churches—emphasis on very—measure anything beyond attendance, donations, square footage, number of programs and size of staff. None of that necessarily reflects life transformation.[7]

FEEL GOOD GOSPEL

Another "ear-tickling" messenger who has emerged in our day is a certain preacher whose endearing and disarming personality has won the hearts of the 30,000 people who attend his church every weekend. His unrelenting message of encouragement has landed his book on the top of the New York Times' Best Seller List. He regularly packs out stadiums of people willing to pay $10 to hear his motivational messages. Although he is extremely careful not to offend his listeners,

---

* This is not to say that all large churches are teaching falsehood. I know of large churches which are biblically sound and are preaching the truth.

his brand of Christianity is slightly different from that of the traditional "seeker-sensitive" teachers. He teaches that God's main concern is to bless people's lives in every possibly way:

> "We're all about building people up. We're all about helping people reach their full potential. We don't push some kind of religion…all we push is joy and peace and victory through Jesus Christ…We've heard a lot about the judgment of God and what we can't do and what's going to keep us out of heaven. But it's time people start hearing about the goodness of God, about a God that loves them. A God that believes in them. A God that wants to help them. That's our message…"[8]

What could be wrong with joyfully leading people into "victory through Jesus Christ?" There would be nothing wrong with it if that was truly happening. Unfortunately, a peek below the surface exposes a rotten theological foundation.

One man who has concerns about him is Dr. Terry Watkins who writes, "In well over 25 hours of preaching that I listened to this year, Jesus was almost never mentioned, and when he was mentioned, it was in a perfunctory prayer in the last minute. Sin, the Cross, the atonement? Not there."[9]

A couple of years ago this successful mega-pastor was interviewed by Larry King on CNN. The following is a smattering of the exchange between the two. For the sake of space, I have cut into the conversation and only included relevant dialog.[†] I have also included a running commentary on these questions and answers by Dr. Watkins.

> <u>King</u>: What if you're Jewish or Muslim, you don't accept Christ at all?

---

† I have the entire transcript of this program in my possession. In spite of the fact that I only extrapolated pertinent portions, what is provided to the reader accurately reflects the tenor of the interview.

Positive Preacher: You know, I'm very careful about saying who would and wouldn't go to heaven. I don't know...

Watkins: At this point, even Larry King appears surprised by [his] answer. Then Larry tosses [him] a "soft-ball" to explain his previous answer. And again [he] openly denies that Jesus Christ is the ONLY way of salvation.

King: If you believe, you have to believe in Christ? They're wrong, aren't they?

Positive Preacher: Well, I don't know if I believe they're wrong. I believe here's what the Bible teaches and from the Christian faith this is what I believe. But I just think that only God will judge a person's heart. I spent a lot of time in India with my father. I don't know all about their religion. But I know they love God. And I don't know. I've seen their sincerity. So I don't know. I know for me, and what the Bible teaches, I want to have a relationship with Jesus.

Watkins: Again [he] denies the redemptive work of the Lord Jesus Christ. Notice, he praises the pagan, false-religion of India as "I know they love God." Unbelievable. I'm sure some reading this are thinking, "Well, maybe Larry caught [him] flat footed. Maybe [he] wasn't prepared." If [he] only had been given another chance to testify of the redemptive work of the Lord Jesus Christ, he'd get it straightened out. [He] did get another chance. . .

After Larry King opened the phone lines, a concerned Christian asks [him] to clarify his previous statement.

Caller: I'm wondering, though, why you side-stepped

Larry's earlier question about how we get to heaven? The Bible clearly tells us that Jesus is the way, the truth and the life and the only way to the Father is through him. That's not really a message of condemnation but of truth.

Positive Preacher: Yes, I would agree with her. I believe that.

King: So then a Jew is not going to heaven?

Positive Preacher: No. Here's my thing, Larry, is I can't judge somebody's heart. You know? Only God can look at somebody's heart, and so—I don't know. To me, it's not my business to say, you know, this one is or this one isn't. I just say, here's what the Bible teaches and I'm going to put my faith in Christ. And I just—think it's wrong when you go around saying, you're saying you're not going, you're not going, you're not going, because it's not exactly my way. I'm just...

King: But you believe your way.

Positive Preacher: I believe my way. I believe my way with all my heart.

King: But for someone who doesn't share it is wrong, isn't he?

Positive Preacher: Well, yes. Well, I don't know if I look at it like that. I would present my way, but I'm just going to let God be the judge of that. I don't know. I don't know.

King: So you make no judgment on anyone?

Positive Preacher: No. But I...

Watkins: And here Larry really tosses [him] a soft-ball. How about a God-defying atheist? And again, [he] will not confess that Jesus Christ is the ONLY way of salvation.

King: But you're not fire and brimstone, right? You're not pound the decks and hell and damnation?

Positive Preacher: No. That's not me. It's never been me...I just—I don't believe in that. I don't believe—maybe it was for a time. But I don't have it in my heart to condemn people. I'm there to encourage them. I see myself more as a coach, as a motivator to help them experience the life God has for us.

Watkins: Friend, the greatest "fire and brimstone" preacher that ever lived was the Lord Jesus! He preached about hell more than any other subject...{This man} may sound pious and sweet to say, "I don't have it in my heart to condemn people," but according to the Lord Jesus, they are already condemned...Friend, if we believe the Bible it is our duty and decency to warn people about hell! Warning someone of the fires of eternal hell is not condemning them—it is just the opposite—we are trying to keep them from being condemned in hell!

King: How about issues that the church has feelings about? Abortion? Same-sex marriages?

Positive Preacher: Yeah. You know what, Larry? I don't go there. I just...

King: You have thoughts, though.

Positive Preacher: I have thoughts. I just, you know, I don't think that a same-sex marriage is the way God intended it to be. I don't think abortion is the best. I think there are other, you know, a better way to live your life. But I'm not going to condemn those people. I tell them all the time our church is open for everybody.

Watkins: Again, Larry appears surprised at [his] waffling. Larry allows [him] to clarify his confusing position. And again [he] blatantly contradicts the words of the Lord Jesus Christ.

King: You don't call them sinners?

Positive Preacher: I don't.

King: Is that a word you don't use?

Positive Preacher: I don't use it. I never thought about it. But I probably don't. But most people already know what they're doing wrong. When I get them to church I want to tell them that you can change. There can be a difference in your life. So I don't go down the road of condemning.‡

Watkins: The word "sin" occurs in the King James Bible over 830 times! [10]

I don't know how we could possibly find a more definitive picture of people accumulating to "themselves teachers in accordance to their own desires." (II Timothy 4:3)

---

‡ It should also be noted that the "Positive Preacher," after apparently being overwhelmed with complaints about his performance, issued an apology on his website. One of the things he said was, "I was unclear on the very thing in which I have dedicated my life." Dr. Watkins' response: "He was not UNCLEAR. He was crystal clear. He consistently and clearly rejected that the Lord Jesus Christ was the ONLY way of salvation! We're not talking about a 'babe in Christ.' We are talking about the pastor of the largest church in the nation!"

David Wilkerson is a man who has been around long enough to see the different trends move through the Church during the past half-century. He is also concerned about what he is seeing in the 21st Century Church:

Frankly, I'm shocked at the hardness I see in so many Christians today, people who were once so on fire. These same believers loved to pray and be in God's house. They loved godly reproof and were stirred deeply by the prophetic words they heard. But now they're too busy to seek God. And their love for Jesus is growing colder by the day.

Such people won't stand for any sort of preaching that convicts them. They prefer to hear a half-hour sermon once a week that builds up their self-esteem or helps them become successful...

Why do so many once zealous Christians now turn away from godly reproof? Why is there such judicial blindness? And why does the self-centered, money-focused, wealth gospel entrap so many churches and believers?

One reason is that a growing number of ministers today have drifted from the preaching of the Cross. The message of the poor, homeless, suffering, bleeding Christ has become an offense. The call to sacrifice—to take up a cross to embrace rejection for Jesus' sake, to become a living sacrifice, to die to self, to repent, to become humble, to crucify the flesh—all of these topics are avoided by preachers of the gospel of happiness and wealth. And all apostolic warnings to be ready for Christ's coming—to trim our lamps, to prepare to meet the Bridegroom, to wake up and redeem the time because the hour is late and because he's coming only for those who look for and love his appearance—all of this is now silenced.[11]

THE MESSAGE OF THE CROSS

If there is one thing that is certain about Satan it is that he will continually try to cheapen the gospel and offer in its place a cut-rate version of his own. Yes, the devil offers a gospel that makes no demands, expects no sacrifice, and yields no eternal rewards—except eternal separation from God!

True Christianity has a value and preciousness of which these spiritual amateurs know nothing. When I think of all of the true saints down through the ages who have earnestly sought God with all their hearts; who have faced "the dark night of the soul" to come into a real relationship with Christ; who have overcome the lusts of their flesh rather than cater to them; who have bravely resisted the enticements of the world; who have humbled themselves before God and man; who have selflessly laid down their lives in Christ's service; who have spent long hours on their knees interceding for lost souls; what am I to think of the cheap, self-centered "Christianity" these hucksters peddle?

Yes, the emblem of our religion is the Cross—the very thing the "feel good" preachers and "seeker-sensitive" pastors avoid at any cost. This is precisely what the Apostle Paul was referring to when he wrote, "For the word of the cross is foolishness to those who are perishing, but to us who are being saved it is the power of God." (I Corinthians 1:18) What they don't seem to understand is that without the Cross, there is no divine blessing, no forgiveness and no salvation. It is all an illusion.

Could it be that behind the plastic smiles, shallow personalities and $2,500 suits these are spiritual cowards who are in it for themselves? Is it possible that they don't understand the Cross because they have never been to it themselves? Are these men "enemies of the cross?" (Philippians 3:18) Could they be leading multitudes into hell? Are they the ones Paul was referring to when he said that there would be end time teachers who are, "deceiving and being deceived?" (II Timothy 3:13) Only

God knows the answer to such questions. One thing we do know for certain because Jesus said it: "It is inevitable that stumbling blocks come, but woe to him through whom they come!" (Luke 17:1)

My dear reader, can I interject a personal message here? I have purposely pounded away at the hawkers of this false gospel with my words because so much is at stake: thousands of souls stand at the brink of eternal destruction. I am not trying to be harsh; I am attempting to expose the lies that are being propagated in our day.

And how about you? Perhaps it would be wise to consider if their message has affected your perspectives about Christianity in any way. Dear one, over and over again end-time Christians are warned, "Do not be deceived!" (e.g. Matthew 24:4, 5, 11, 24) "The world is full of deceivers," wrote Adam Clarke, "and it is only by taking heed to the counsel of Christ that even his followers can escape being ruined by them."[12]

Let the Word of God guide you into Truth. One thing that might be helpful is to simply sit down and read through the book of John. Consider the way Jesus interacted with the people He encountered. Compare the way He dealt with people to what you hear from Christian radio, see on Christian television or read at Christian bookstores. Just because someone is financially able to purchase prime radio time or have his books prominently displayed does not mean that he is accurately representing Jesus Christ. Remember: It is Scripture, not the success of marketing ploys, that establishes truth.

The painful fact of the matter is that there are many false teachers at work in the Church today. Sin and deception seem to be peaking just as the Bible foretells. Is it possible that we really are approaching the End?

"Is not the Church in its present state, a standing, public, perpetual denial of the gospel? Does it not stand out before the world, as a living, unanswerable contradiction of the gospel; and do more to harden sinners and lead them into a spirit of caviling and infidelity, than all the efforts of professed infidels from the beginning of the world to the present day?" ↭ Charles Finney[1]

"The earth is ripening, and men's characters are rotting to the uttermost degree of corruption. This is the age of villainy, the chosen era of shams, lies, and hypocrisies, and we must expect to see more and more of the boilings over of the sink of iniquity, which lies in human nature. Be not startled, if in these last days there should be seen whole herds of wolves in sheep's clothing, deceivers and defamers of the church, for even so have we been warned by the voice of God...
O deceitful professor, will not the Lord be avenged upon you for this? Is it nothing to make Jesus' name the drunkard's song? Nothing to make the enemy blaspheme? O hardened man, tremble, for this shall not go unpunished."
↭ Charles Spurgeon[2]

Chapter Fifteen:
FALLEN LEADERS

*"You also outwardly seem to people to be just
and upright but inside you are full of pretense
and lawlessness and iniquity."*
(Matthew 23:28 AMP)

A few days ago I was talking to a dear African-American lady. She was confiding to me that she had evidence that for several years her pastor had been sexually involved with a number of women in his mega-church. This was not the chitchat of a gossip, but the painful admission that the man she had spent many hours interceding for was given over to unrepentant immorality. "Brother Steve," she told me earnestly, "He is such an awesome man of God!"

When she made that statement I immediately interrupted her. "Joyce*, he is NOT an awesome man of God! If he were, he wouldn't be involved in such behavior. He may be gifted, but he is not a man of God."

For all her sincerity and godliness, Joyce had bought into the common thinking of our day that a person's abilities as a leader and speaker determine his level of godliness.

Without question, Church history has had its share of religious imposters and fallen leaders, but there has never been

---

* A pseudonym.

a time when so many have been brought into public disrepute as in our day. Perhaps you have lost track of some of the headlines that have brought disgrace to the name of Christ in our time. Consider what we have witnessed in the past twenty years.

In 1987, Jim Bakker was forced to resign his position as president of the vast PTL television network after being confronted with rumors that he had had sexual relations with Jessica Hahn. He was later convicted of fraud and conspiracy charges for illegally soliciting millions of dollars from followers and was forced to spend five years in federal prison.

The following year, Jimmy Swaggart confessed to moral failure on national television after he was photographed going into a motel with a known prostitute. He was defrocked by the Assemblies of God when he refused to submit to their restoration process. Three years later, he was stopped for a traffic violation in a known red-light district with a woman who told police she was a prostitute.

In 1992, David Hocking, pastor of the church at Biola University, whose sermons were featured on a national radio program, was forced to resign his position when it came to light that he had engaged in sexual behavior with a woman in his car.

In 1993, Christian author, pastor, and seminary professor Mel White, perhaps best known for ghost-writing Jerry Falwell's autobiography, acknowledged that he had been involved in homosexuality for many years. White went on to found a pro-homosexual organization and has been active in the leadership of the Metropolitan Community Churches.

In 1998, Paul Crouch, founder and president of Trinity Broadcasting Network, was forced to reach an out of court settlement with a known drug addict who claimed that the two of them had had homosexual relations. Although he attempted to hide the allegations, Crouch never acknowledged them to be true.

The next year, Henry Lyons, president of the National Baptist Convention USA, was forced to resign his position when his wife set fire to the mansion he secretly shared with his mistress. He was later sentenced to five years in prison after being found guilty of swindling companies out of millions of dollars.

In 2000, Mike Trout, vice-president of Focus on the Family and co-host of their tremendously popular radio show, was forced to resign after admitting to having an ongoing adulterous affair with a woman.

In 2001, Roberts Liardon, author of *God's Generals*, a history of Pentecostal pioneers, confessed to having a homosexual encounter with another man.

In 2003, Earl Paulk, mega-church pastor and president of the International Communion of Charismatic Churches, was forced to settle an out of court case with a woman with whom he had had an affair. That same year, Michael Johnston, one of the leading national spokesmen of the pro-family movement on the issue of homosexuality, confessed to having liaisons with numerous men over a period of nearly two years.

In 2004, "prophet" Paul Cain admitted to alcoholism and to being involved in homosexuality.

In 2006, Ted Haggard, mega-church pastor and president of the National Association of Evangelicals, was exposed for having a three-year sexual affair with a male masseur.

These stories are a matter of public record and are not being mentioned with any intention of dragging the names of these men back "through the mud." I only bring these scandals up to accentuate to the reader the moral condition of the Church in our day.

It should also be noted that at least three of these men have clearly repented. Jim Bakker came clean in his book, *I Was Wrong*. David Hocking worked through his problems under the care of Pastor Chuck Smith. Michael Johnston underwent a grueling two-year restoration process at Pure Life Ministries. While the spiritual status of the others is unknown to the author, we should remember that it is God's heart to restore the repentant sinner.

I wish I could say that the damage was confined to these well known cases. Unfortunately, I have also been personally privy to reports about other nationally known figures who have fallen morally but have managed to keep their escapades under wraps.[†] On top of all of this, there have undoubtedly been thousands of local ministers who have been involved in pornography and sexual sin over the past couple of decades. One can only imagine how much other corruption has yet to surface.

It goes without saying that sexual sin is only one form of spiritual failure. How many other ministers are full of pride, serving selfish interests? How many pastors treat their followers with kindness, but when nobody is looking vent their anger at loved ones? How many are fully given over to the spirit of this world?

As Peter was writing his final epistle, in much the same way as happened with Paul, he seemed to suddenly enter a prophetic mindset when he penned what became the second and third chapters. "Many will follow their sensuality," he wrote, "the way of the truth will be maligned." (II Peter 2:2)

Beloved, if the horrid twenty-year chronology I just outlined isn't a fulfillment of this prophecy, what else could be? If you doubt that all of this hasn't caused the name of Christ to be maligned, just type "religious scandals" into an Internet search engine and see what people are saying about the precious faith Christ purchased with His blood.

This rotten mess plays such a part in the end-times Church that we must examine it in greater detail. As you well know,

---

† I am not at liberty to divulge their identities, nor would it be appropriate to do so in this context. However, I assure you, within their realm of influence these individuals are known nation-wide.

Second Peter 2 and the book of Jude are nearly identical.‡
Apparently, the Lord considered the subject matter so important
that He made certain it was expressed twice. That alone should
cause us to pay special attention to it, considering how many
other important eschatological subjects are only mentioned
once.

In an effort to vivify the reality of what is being expressed
about the end-times, let's take a look at some of the important
terms Peter employed.

DENY

"...there will also be false teachers among you,
who will secretly introduce destructive heresies, even
denying the Master who bought them..." (II Peter 2:1)

The use of the word *deny* (Gk. *arneomai*) to describe these
men is significant because it dispels the false notions that merely
confessing Christ with words brings salvation and that denying
Christ necessitates a verbal renunciation of Him. The truth is that
we confess or deny the Lord through the way we live our lives.

Paul made a very interesting statement in his epistle to
Titus. I will use the Amplified to bring out the full meaning of
his words:

To the pure [*in heart and conscience*] all things are pure,
but to the defiled and corrupt (Gk. *miaino*) and unbelieving
nothing is pure; their very minds and consciences are
defiled and polluted (Gk. *miaino*). They profess to know
God [*to recognize, perceive, and be acquainted with Him*], but
deny (Gk. *arneomai*) and disown and renounce Him
by what they do; they are detestable and loathsome,
unbelieving and disobedient and disloyal and rebellious,

---

‡ Most commentators I have read believe that Peter wrote his epistle first and Jude borrowed
from it.

and [*they are*] unfit and worthless for good work (deed or enterprise) of any kind. (Titus 1:15-16 AMP)

Do you remember the term *miasmos* in Chapter Eleven? It signifies corruption and later became used in the English language to describe the fumes arising from a noxious swamp. *Miasmos* is a derivative of the primary verb *miaino*. These false teachers crawled out of the same swamp of selfishness and corruption. They name the name of Christ, but what they do when nobody is looking is a de facto renunciation of all that Christ stands for. No wonder their perception of the Christian life is so skewed.

No, they would never verbally deny Christ; in fact their entire ministries are built (however superficially) around the premise that Jesus Christ is who He claimed to be. But the way they live their lives is a denial of everything Jesus stood for.

SELF-WILLED, DESPISING AUTHORITY

"They...scorn and despise authority. Presumptuous [and] daring [self-willed and self-loving creatures]!"
(II Peter 2:10 AMP)

Every true believer has a hedge around his life that keeps him within certain boundaries of behavior. When he begins to stray off the narrow way, the Holy Spirit is there to impede his progress. But people differ in how they respond to this divine constraint. The Pulpit Commentary exposes the difference between the person who sees God's will as a bother and the one who sees it as a blessing.

Divine limitations are felt to be irksome to us when our will is in conflict with God's will...But we men on earth live in frequent conflict with our heavenly Father's will. We find the walls to be hard because we fling ourselves upon them. Our chain galls us because we chafe and fret ourselves against it. The wandering sheep is torn by the hedge, while the quiet obedient sheep knows nothing of the briars. When we rebel against God we murmur at his restraints...

Far the highest obedience is not the restraint of our will before God's will, but the assimilation of the two. We learn to will what God wills. Then we keep within the Divine limitations, and yet they cease to be limitations to us. They never touch us because we never attempt nor wish to cross them. Here lies the secret of peace as well as of holiness. So lofty an attainment can only be reached through that oneness with Christ of which he speaks when he prays that his disciples may be one with him and the Father, as he is one with the Father (John 17:21).[3]

Those who make themselves the Lord's spokesmen should be the first to embrace His will, but alas, they are often the ones who say in their hearts, "We do not want this man to reign over us." (Luke 19:14) They become like those who shake their fists at God and proclaim, "Let us break Their bands [*of restraint*] asunder and cast Their cords [*of control*] from us." (Psalm 2:3 AMP) They want what they want and will often do whatever it takes to get it.

I should also mention that people don't just "fall" into sin, as if they were walking along a path in the dark and suddenly— through no fault of their own—fall into a hole. There are definite reasons why it happens. By the time a minister has gotten to the point that he is willing to be sexually involved with another person outside his marriage, he has lived in self-will and self-indulgence for a long time. The sin he eventually indulges in is simply one more step in a long series of acts of rebellion against God.

DARING

"Daring..." (II Peter 2:10)

Consider some of the synonyms that come forth from other Bible translations: "Presumptuous and daring" (AMP); "ready to take chances" (BBE); and, "bold and arrogant." (NIV) Strong's Bible Dictionary labels him as "a *daring (audacious)* man."

These various terms would certainly seem to apply to some of the fallen ministers mentioned above. Did Jimmy Swaggart really believe that he wouldn't be recognized as he cruised the red-light district a few short miles from his worldwide headquarters? What was especially audacious of him was calling Jim Bakker a "blemish" on the Church, while at the same time indulging in his own acts of uncleanness.

Ted Haggard showed little more wisdom or constraint. *Time* magazine tells about a documentary where he is shown telling a crowd, "We don't have to have a debate about what we think about homosexual activity. It's written in the Bible." A few minutes later, he "looks mockingly into the camera to say, 'I think I know what you did last night. If you send me a thousand dollars, I won't tell your wife.' The crowd responds with peals of laughter. Then he says with a wide smile, 'If you use any of this, I'll sue you.'" [4]

Michael Johnston tells the story of being a keynote speaker at a huge pro-family event where his rousing words brought 2,000 Christian activists to their feet in applause. After finishing his speech, he went to his hotel room where he engaged in sex with two men.

The truth is that any pastor or minister who becomes involved in sexual sin is taking a huge gamble of getting caught and ruining his reputation. Even worse, "...because of them the way of the truth will be maligned." (II Peter 2:2) Who can measure the harm these men have done to people who are considering following Jesus Christ or are just beginning their journey?

SPRINGS WITHOUT WATER, MISTS DRIVEN BY A STORM

"These people are as useless as dried-up springs
of water or as clouds blown away by the
wind–promising much and delivering nothing."
(II Peter 2:17 NLT)

Both of these metaphors describe the same phenomenon and mirror what Jesus said about a false teacher being a "bad tree [that] bears bad fruit." (Matthew 7:17) All three of these similes were used to illustrate the fact that people go to religious leaders to receive spiritual nourishment. The hungry soul goes to the tree looking for some luscious fruit to eat and finds that the fruit is inedible. The hot and thirsty traveler rushes to the spring only to discover that it is dry. The farmer waits for the showers to water his crops, but the clouds roll by without producing any moisture. In each case the lesson is obvious: These teachers have no spiritual substance which hungry souls can draw upon. When they teach, their words are empty and lifeless.

Any person—no matter how gifted, eloquent or charismatic— can only be used in the kingdom of God to the extent that he is filled with and controlled by the Holy Ghost. Without the aid of the Spirit, he is but a spring without water.

As I said, there are many ministers in the U.S. who are regularly involved in pornography and/or sexual sin. They do not realize the danger they are in. There is a scene in the movie, *Fellowship of the Ring*, where Aragorn asks Frodo if he is frightened. Frodo responds, "Yes." Aragorn then ominously says what I want to say to these frolicking ministers: "You are not nearly frightened enough. I know what hunts you." A devil is stalking them, luring them and dragging them into ever greater darkness. The "power of the ring" is growing stronger in its grip on them. If I sound like I am being overly dramatic, the truth is that I am not being nearly dramatic enough: they have every reason to fear.

Consider what the Word of God promises to these unrepentant false teachers:

- "...whose punishment has been ready for a long time and their destruction is watching for them;" (II Peter 2:3 BBE)
- "For if God did not have pity for the angels who did evil, but sent them down into hell, to be kept in chains of eternal night till they were judged;" (II Peter 2:4 BBE)
- "The Lord is able to keep evil-doers under punishment till the day of judging;" (II Peter 2:9 BBE)
- "...for whom the eternal night is kept in store;" (II Peter 2:17 BBE)

I will never forget the time when I confronted a leader of a respected Christian organization about his unrepentant sexual sin. His wife had confided to me about his secret sin and I had been laboring in prayer for him for some time. You must understand that I did and still do love this man. One morning, I felt the Lord gave me a strong warning for him from the first chapter of Proverbs. Sadly, he rejected this word and, as far as I know, continued on in his sin. Nevertheless, these words are an ominous reminder to us all of what is at stake:

> Come here and listen to me! I'll pour out the spirit of wisdom upon you, and make you wise. I have called you so often but still you won't come. I have pleaded, but all in vain. For you have spurned my counsel and reproof...
>
> When a storm of terror surrounds you, and when you are engulfed by anguish and distress, then I will not answer your cry for help. It will be too late though you search for me ever so anxiously.

For you closed your eyes to the facts and did not choose to reverence and trust the Lord, and you turned your back on me, spurning my advice.

That is why you must eat the bitter fruit of having your own way, and experience the full terrors of the pathway you have chosen. For you turned away from me—to death; your own complacency will kill you. (Proverbs 1:23-32 LIV)

There will always be those who will not respond to the call of the Lord. They are willful rebels who are bent on having their own way.

Christian leaders like this are making the Cross of Jesus Christ a mockery to the world. The real tragedy of stories like these is that instead of drawing people to the lovely Savior, these impostors are driving them away. "Many will follow their sensuality," Peter predicted, "and because of them the way of the truth will be maligned." (II Peter 2:2)

While it is true that there are tares in the field, it is also just as true that there is wheat as well. These children of God long to know Jesus in a greater way. They are looking forward to the coming of the Lord. They are the Virgins who are ready to meet the Bridegroom.

"[Christ] will not be seen in the travail of His souls until in all His purity, beauty, power and glory He is seen in His saints...Oh for that day when Jesus shall be fully seen in us!"
❧ George Bowen[1]

"Oh, that the Lord would arise, and sweep away the deadly errors which now pollute the very air! We long for the time when the powers of darkness shall be baffled...and when the true Church shall be revealed in all her purity and beauty as the Bride of Christ, and the apostate church shall be put away once for all and for ever." ❧ Charles Spurgeon[2]

"There will come a time when My anointed will walk in freedom, having no bonds or entanglements with the world. It will be a time when those devoted to Me and Me alone will rise above all of the restrictions and sin that have held My bride captive...I have told you of a salvation to be revealed in the last time. I have told you of a great harvest. Now I am about to equip those whom I can trust. Be part of My bride. The time is short."
❧ Jim Corbett (From Our Father's Heart)[3]

Chapter Sixteen:
THE GREAT OUTPOURING

"It will come about after this that I will pour out My Spirit on all mankind; and your sons and daughters will prophesy, your old men will dream dreams, your young men will see visions." (Joel 2:28)

Revival has always been a part of God's dealings with mankind. Under normal circumstances, people are led to Christ through the witnessing of an acquaintance, the anointed preaching of a minister or an inspired book. However, there are also those occasions when God supernaturally moves in communities.

Four characteristics mark these situations as revival. First, the presence of the Holy Spirit is manifested in a very powerful way. Second, God's people are spiritually energized and invigorated. Third, large numbers of people become radically converted. Fourth, a good deal of the community at large is affected by this great influx of spiritual energy.

This certainly occurred during the Old Testament period. The Hebrew word *chayah* is used 241 times in the O.T. and is variously translated as *revive, revived, quicken, life* and *recover* (to name some of the more prominent usages). "A strict definition of revive," Glenn Meldrum says, "means to bring back to life that which is dead, or to resuscitate that which is dying. *Chayah*

directly speaks of God reviving, or bringing back to life, a person, people or nation that is spiritually dead or dying."[4]

There are a number of such spiritual awakenings recorded in Scripture. Most of these occurred when the people of Israel returned to God from a backslidden state.* However, a clear-cut example of revival happened in Nineveh when the prophet Jonah warned the pagan city of impending judgment if they did not repent. God moved mightily among those Assyrian people and they cried out for mercy to the great Jehovah of Israel.

This spiritual phenomenon carried forth into the New Testament as well. The birth of the Christian Church occurred on the Day of Pentecost, when the Holy Spirit was poured out in a dramatic way upon 120 people who were waiting on God. Over 3,000 people were saved that day! This revival received new impetus when Saul of Tarsus received a revelation of Christ on the road to Damascus. It seems that nearly everywhere he preached, the power of God moved upon people's hearts. For instance, he wrote to the Thessalonians: "For our gospel did not come to you in word only, but also in power and in the Holy Spirit and with full conviction." (I Thessalonians 1:5) He told them that they "turned to God from idols to serve a living and true God." (II Thessalonians 1:9) He also said of his time with the Thessalonians that the word of God "spread rapidly and [was] glorified." (II Thessalonians 3:1)

While there were certain courageous men such as Chrysostom and Savonarola whose fearless preaching during the Dark Ages brought about noteworthy results, for the most part, no large scale revivals took place during that time.

The Lord used John Wesley and George Whitefield to bring about the Great Awakening of the 18th Century. Jonathan Edwards was another key figure of this great move of God. It was said that when Edwards gave his famous message, *Sinners in the Hands of an Angry God*, people cried out in terror, clutching

---

* Some examples of this can be found in I Samuel 7, II Chronicles 29, Nehemiah 9, etc.

at the pews in fear that the floor beneath them would open and there would be nothing to stop them from sliding into hell.†

In the early 1800's, God used Charles Finney as an instrument to bring about the Second Great Awakening. It has been said that he exuded so much power that people would often break down weeping when he entered a room.

One dramatic experience occurred not long after he was ordained. He arrived in an area of upstate New York known then as Hell's Acres because of its wickedness, where he was invited to preach by the deacon of a small Baptist church.

> The Spirit of God came upon me with such power that it was like opening a battery upon them. For more than an hour, and perhaps for an hour and a half, the word of God came through me to them in a manner that I could see was carrying all before it. It was a fire and a hammer breaking the rock; and as the sword that was piercing to the dividing asunder of soul and spirit. I saw that a general conviction was spreading over the whole congregation. Many of them could not hold up their heads.[5]

Not long after this happened, he preached at another church in the area. He used as his text, "Up, get out of this place, for the Lord will destroy the city." (Genesis 19:14) Finney warned them that God was going to send judgment upon them because of their sin. The people were becoming increasingly angry with him—to the point that he feared they would attack him. He continued preaching, however, when suddenly "an awful solemnity" came over the people.

---

† Skeptics and lifeless, religious people have attempted to explain away this sermon by saying that Edwards terrified simple-minded people into conversions. It is just as Paul himself said, "A natural man does not accept the things of the Spirit of God, for they are foolishness to him; and he cannot understand them..." (I Corinthians 2:14)

"The congregation began to fall from their seats in every direction, and cried for mercy. If I had had a sword in each hand, I could not have cut them off their seats as fast as they fell. Indeed nearly the whole congregation were either on their knees or prostrate, I should think, in less than two minutes from this first shock that fell upon them. Every one prayed for himself, who was able to speak at all."

He was unable to continue. The people were crying out for mercy and in such agony, they no longer heard anything he said.[6]

Apparently, half a million people came to the Lord through Charles Finney's preaching alone. This revival soon spread across the Northeast as the harvest grew greater.

The early part of the 20th Century brought about another dramatic outpouring of God's Spirit. According to Glenn Meldrum, over 5 million people were saved during the revivals that occurred worldwide between 1903 and 1910.[7] One of those revivalists was Jonathon Goforth, a Presbyterian missionary to China. Another missionary who was present described what happened at one of his services:

Then began a meeting the like of which I had never seen before, nor wish to see again unless in God's sight it is absolutely necessary. Every sin a human being can commit was publicly confessed that night. Pale and trembling with emotion, in agony of mind and body, guilty souls, standing in the white light of their judgment, saw themselves as God saw them. Their sins rose up in all their vileness, till shame and grief and self-loathing took complete possession; pride was driven out, the face of man forgotten. Looking up to heaven, to Jesus whom they had betrayed, they smote themselves and cried out with bitter wailing: "Lord, Lord, cast us not away forever!" Everything else was forgotten, nothing else mattered. The scorn of men, the penalty of the law, even death itself seemed of small consequence if only God forgave.[8]

In 1949, a powerful revival broke out on the Hebrides Islands off the coast of Scotland under the preaching of Duncan Campbell.

A mighty conviction of sin seized the community. Deep, heart-felt repentance flowed through the town as a flood on dry ground. Whether in the open streets, or in the midst of a dance hall, people fell to their knees, pleading forgiveness from God. "Fear gripped people everywhere...A great crowd surged around the church when suddenly, as the preacher came to the door, the Spirit of God swept among them as a great wind. They gripped each other's arms in deadly fear and terror and, in agony of soul, they trembled and wept, and many fell to the ground under deep conviction of sin."[9]

Kathy and I have witnessed this same kind of heavy conviction in meetings where the presence of God filled the atmosphere. But we have also experienced His presence in our personal lives as well. In 1997, Kathy had a divine visitation in our home. She describes what happened:

All of the sudden I knew that Jesus was in the room. Instantly I fell on my face and began weeping uncontrollably. He was so near to me it was almost like He was touching me. I just stayed on the floor. I would try to get up but couldn't. For the next two or three weeks, every time I went into that room in the morning, He was there waiting for me, His love filling the atmosphere. During those encounters I felt strongly compelled to pray for my husband. I would go into very intense intercession for Steve. There were times when I simply knew it was the Holy Spirit praying through me on my husband's behalf.[10]

I have shared these tidbits in an attempt to establish what it is like when God supernaturally visits mankind. Revival and supernatural outpourings have been just as much a part of Church history as the Reformation. The Christian Church was birthed in revival and I fully believe it will consummate its earthly existence in the greatest revival this world has ever witnessed.‡

THE GREAT OUTPOURING

When revival falls upon a community, the first reaction people experience is to become acutely aware of their sin. True revival is always accompanied by deep and pervasive repentance. Lives become radically transformed. Unbelievers— sometimes the worst of sinners—get saved and walk away from their ungodly lifestyles forever. Hypocrites experience true conversion. Furthermore, even true believers who have grown cold become ignited in their love for God. On the other hand,

---

‡ While I felt I should touch upon this subject as part of the purpose of this book, it would require a book in itself to lay the proper biblical foundation for why I believe this. I should also mention that there are a number of teachings available under the term "Latter Rain." I have found teachings that I would consider solid biblical exposition of Scripture but others that are downright "super-spiritual" nonsense. The Assemblies of God developed a position paper entitled, "Resolution 16, A Return to Biblical Integrity," which says in part: "But along with the genuine move of the Spirit often come teachings and practices which, if not discerned and corrected, will turn the genuine move of God into shallow and misguided emotional displays. Within teachings that add to or depart from biblical truth, there is usually a kernel of truth that gets buried under the chaff of human additions and unusual interpretations of Scripture. Though we dare not inadvertently quench the Spirit's work in changing lives and calling the church back to its first love and passion, we must speak out with words of caution when departure from Scripture threatens the ongoing life and stability of local churches." I think these are wise words for all Christians to heed.

those who only have emotional experiences may become excited for a time but do not change. True revival reaches deeply within people's hearts and sets them on a new course of life.

The world has seen these divine visitations from time to time, but, for the most part, they have been confined to local areas or regions. One can only imagine what it will be like when God pours out His Spirit around the world.

The great revival that Scripture predicts will not only fill people with the love of God in a tremendous way, but it will also infuse believers with His power. People with a track record of maintaining control over their lives and only allowing God limited access to their hearts find such ideas ridiculous. They are so accustomed to living with an earthbound and temporal mindset that such talk seems like so much nonsense to them. Even many sincere believers have confined God to such a rigid box that they refuse to believe He actually moves outside of their finite conceptions.

But dear ones, we must ask ourselves if we really believe what the Bible says. Consider some of the seemingly farfetched stories the Bible purports to have occurred. Samson pulled loose the gates of the Gaza city walls—which probably weighed several hundred pounds—and carried them about 20 miles to the top of a mountain. (Judges 16:3) When King Ahab drove his chariot at least ten miles to beat an approaching thunderstorm, Elijah actually outran him on foot. (I Kings 18:46) When three Jews refused to worship an image to King Nebuchadnezzar, he threw them into a blazing furnace and they were completely untouched by the flames. (Daniel 3:25) When Jonah was thrown overboard during a storm on the Mediterranean Sea, a giant fish swallowed him alive and deposited him on the seashore unharmed three days later. (Jonah 2:10) When Philip baptized an Ethiopian eunuch, the Holy Spirit physically "snatched" him away, depositing him nearly thirty miles away. (Acts 8:39-40) When a believer named Tabitha died, Peter prayed over her and she was raised from the dead. (Acts 9:41)

Answer this question honestly: If you would have been alive during the time of any of these experiences, would you have believed that they really happened, or would you think the person had made it up?

Many express belief in these stories, but the truth is that they are little more than ancient fables to them. Anyone can say he believes God worked supernaturally long ago, but his faith is not tested until he is asked if the Lord can and will work in such ways here and now. I believe the Lord does work supernaturally now, but His power has been greatly limited by our lack of faith. Nevertheless, when God pours out His Spirit upon mankind, these kinds of miracles will become commonplace among His people.

A WHITE STONE

It was back in the early 90's that I came to the conviction that the people of God in the Last Days would return to the miraculous living and deep love that was so manifest in the Early Church. I have met very few people who share this belief, so imagine my surprise when I discovered a novel which perfectly describes the very thing I have long believed! The story of *A White Stone* is set in the Last Days and describes what happens when a group of street people have a powerful encounter with God and live out the very kind of Christianity that is described in the book of Acts. The following extract is an overview of life during that time:

> Those who heard the call of the bride, and responded with repentance for their adherence to a self-indulgent gospel, thrived during these times. Never opposing government and never coming against anyone who did not believe as they did, the real church of Jesus Christ was equipped to touch and help many lives, providing basic life needs, even during the hardest of times.

Even though they embraced all, they were labeled as bigots for believing that Jesus was the only way to God as the Bible stated. All real harm—eternal harm—could not touch them as they walked above man's way of doing things and only in the ways of God. Their response to any form of opposition was always to love deeper and forgive more earnestly so that the keeping power of the Holy Spirit would envelop them.

Those who did not respond to God's call to intimacy found themselves unable to grasp real peace in this time of great need. Fear, worry and anger were the constant companions of the children of God who saw fit to do their own thing, maintaining their own agenda when the purifying call went out years before. Now, the spiritual "tools" necessary to walk in love in the worst of situations, as Jesus did, were unavailable to them. Many died in the subsequent holocaust, cursing those who killed them and losing the opportunity to be a witness of the power of the cross. Those who embraced the life that had been chosen for them knew that they had been raised up for a time such as this. Nothing mattered but to love and serve the Lord and others, until their allotted time on this earth ended.

As the purifying fire intensified, it strengthened those who saw their lives as God's property. They understood the plans of God because they knew Him intimately. It did not matter whether their God would miraculously intervene in any given situation or whether death by the violence of others' actions would take place to those who were given the faith that Jesus had—faith that caused them to lay their lives in the hands of their loving Father, trusting that He would deliver them should He choose to. If not, it meant in the truest sense "to live is Christ; to die is gain."[11]

"The Church that is man-managed instead of God governed is doomed to failure. A ministry that is college-trained but not Spirit-filled works no miracles." ∾ Samuel Chadwick[1]

"The only escape in the last days will be into God." ∾ Rex Andrews

"The wise virgins will come to the light and be perfected in love. The foolish virgins, the harlot church, will scoff and mock with controversial questions and disputes about words. The false teachers who oppose restoration to God's real church today will be completely cut off unless they repent! Those who will not repent and come to God's light will become furious and angry as they see people leaving their fleshly kingdoms to become a part of the remnant of restoration." ∾ Milton Green[2]

"It is the doom of the apostate church on earth that evokes this burst of praise in heaven [referring to the scene depicted in Revelation 19]." ∾ Sir Robert Anderson[3]

Chapter Seventeen:

THE FALL OF THE APOSTATE CHURCH

"How long, O Lord? Will You be angry forever?
Shall Your jealousy [which cannot endure a divided
allegiance] burn like fire?" (Psalm 79:5 AMP)

B y the First Century, true faith in Jehovah had been replaced by dead ritualism. People had learned to live an outward religious life, while keeping their hearts far from God. Those who showed the greatest aptitude at gaining the admiration of others rose through the ranks of Judaism. Religious journeymen controlled the sacred halls of the great Temple. A terrible religious system had become entrenched among God's people.

It was into the world of the Pharisees and Sadducees that John the Baptist was born. He came from a long line of Jewish priests and was, himself, trained from childhood to follow in his father's priestly footsteps. But at some point John separated himself from this religious system and went out into the wilderness to find God for himself.

When he was 30-years-old, John burst upon the scene with the same abruptness as Elijah had some nine centuries before. Like his Old Testament predecessor, John isolated himself from the religious system of his day and preached with fearlessness toward it. His life of self-denial was a visible protest against the corruption of indulgence that had overtaken God's people.

The Baptist's life work was fairly simple. He was to prepare the way for the Messiah by calling the Jewish people to repent of their hypocrisy and sin. Even the men who controlled the religious system within which he had been raised didn't escape his piercing denunciations.

"You brood of vipers, who warned you to flee from the wrath to come?" He cried out. "Therefore bear fruit in keeping with repentance…The axe is already laid at the root of the trees; therefore every tree that does not bear good fruit is cut down and thrown into the fire." (Matthew 3:7-10) His message was unmistakable: "Your religious system is coming down. If you don't humble yourselves and get right with God you will be destroyed along with it."

"As for me," he continued, "I baptize you with water for repentance, but He who is coming after me…will baptize you with the Holy Spirit and fire. His winnowing fork is in His hand, and He will thoroughly clear His threshing floor; and He will gather His wheat into the barn, but He will burn up the chaff with unquenchable fire." (Matthew 3:11-12) In other words, you can either subject yourself to God's baptism of fire or you will face the eternal fire of judgment.

This was the advent of the long-awaited Messiah—the Son of the living God! His ministry and message were to be characterized by fire. Jesus Christ began His ministry in a fire that remained unabated until His crucifixion some three years later.

But it wasn't until Pentecost that the fire of God burst forth upon the Messiah's followers. "And suddenly there came from heaven a noise like a violent rushing wind, and it filled the whole house where they were sitting. And there appeared to them tongues as of fire distributing themselves, and they rested on each one of them. And they were all filled with the

Holy Spirit and began to speak with other tongues…" (Acts 2:2-
4) Peter was so affected that day that he went out and preached
to the curious spectators who had gathered and led 3,000 souls
into God's kingdom. In fact, what was kindled within those 120
believers that day enabled them to live the rest of their lives in
a red-hot passion for God.

It was also the beginning of the end for the corrupt Jewish
system. When the Jewish leaders rejected the preaching of the
Cross, the system began to deteriorate. Within one generation,
Jerusalem would be plundered, the Temple torn down and most
of the remaining Jews sold into Roman slavery.

THE RETURN OF CHRIST

In a similar way, a religious system has become entrenched
within the modern American Church and has subsequently
spread its perspectives and values around the world. Its
powerbrokers control the lines of communication to the
Christian world. Publishing empires, television networks, radio
station conglomerates and bookstore chains are owned by a
small number of people—many of whom don't even claim to
be Christians.

Within this framework, talented preachers, authors,
counselors, activists and musicians rise to stardom. Among
these, there are sincere, godly leaders whom the Lord has raised
up; but they are intermingled with a horde of hypocrites who
are extremely adept at plying their talents to win followers to
themselves. (Acts 20:29-30)

The competition for readers, listeners and adherents can
be intense in the great realm of American Christendom.
Media personalities are under enormous pressure to gain the
financial support necessary to keep their programs on the
airwaves. Ambitious pastors must tailor their messages and
worship to meet the approval of their congregations. Musicians

must create music that is stimulating. Authors must hold their reader's attention. Anyone with a charismatic personality, natural abilities and a positive message can enjoy tremendous fame and success.*

The desire for success compels many of these religious leaders to carefully avoid topics that might offend followers. By and large, people want to hear positive messages that affirm their lifestyles. Therefore, subjects such as sin, selfishness, worldliness, repentance and so on, are dealt with superficially, or more commonly, they are avoided altogether.

The result is as astounding as it is inescapable: a large percentage of Christians are really not living in a true faith in Christ. Instead, their minds are governed by a deep cynicism toward the things of God. Their belief is academic rather than experiential. They live for this temporal world rather than God's Kingdom. The return of Christ is a nice storyline for intriguing novels and action-packed movies, but the thought of it does not compel them to be spiritually prepared.

All of this has fashioned a corporate perspective that has become deeply-rooted over the years. This great mindset controls its members, dictating acceptable and unacceptable behavior. There is an unwritten code of conduct that is loosely based upon Scripture. Positive behavior (attending church, reading books, listening to Christian radio, etc.) is commended; negative behavior (smoking, drinking, cussing, fornication, etc.) is frowned upon. This superficial perspective ignores what God

---

* I know the System so well because there was a time when I lived for what it offered. With all my heart I wanted to succeed in it. My search for inner significance and outward honor drove me to work tirelessly. I campaigned for my cause. I tried to meet the right people and be on the most popular programs. I fought and struggled to climb the "ladder." I prayed my heart out for God to bless my ministry. I was sincere in my desire to help others, but Self dominated much of my efforts. By 1992, I had appeared on a number of national television and radio programs. Then, just as it seemed I was about to break into something "great," I had a crisis: God began exposing my pride and ambition. Every time I attempted to move forward on my own, I faced His discipline. It became a very painful seven-year period of severe chastisement. Today, I am extremely grateful to the Lord for setting me free of my driving ambition.

sees most clearly—the absence of traits like love, humility and holiness that ought to be growing within the hearts of true believers.

RETURN OF THE FIRE

Jesus Christ will return, but He is going to come *to* His people before He comes *for* His people. He is going to pour out His Spirit upon mankind once again. What happened in Jerusalem on the Day of Pentecost and was somewhat repeated on Azusa Street in Los Angeles a century ago were but precursors of what is yet to come. Once again, the fire of God is going to burn in His people.

Not many Christians have really experienced the fire of God. Most have encountered His presence just enough to feel the glow of His love from a distance. They are like the blind man who feels the slight warmth of a raging bonfire from a distance but thinks he is close to a tiny campfire. They do not understand that if they were to actually draw near to this great Being, they would find that His love is not an ember of affection like they possess for others but an inferno of passion. He will not share His beloved with another: "For the Lord your God is a consuming fire, a jealous God." (Deuteronomy 4:24)

When people draw near to God—whether through their own seeking or by the divine visitation of revival—they will also come face-to-face with His fire. There are a number of inevitable results from such an encounter.

First, God's fire inflames hearts. There is a deadly chill over the heart of man. Only the Holy Spirit can ignite a heart that is cold to the things of God.

Ministers can work up a passion in their preaching or be very zealous about their spiritual activities, but only the Holy Spirit can put fire in their words. The Psalmist said that the Lord makes "his ministers a flaming fire." (Psalm 104:4b KJV) The Lord asked,

"Is not My word like fire?" (Jeremiah 23:29a) When God lays hold of a man, he will live and preach in a divine fervor for souls.

An example of this that comes to mind is when Jeff Colón, the director of the Pure Life Ministries counseling department, went to Pensacola to attend the revival meetings taking place at Brownsville Assembly of God church. He was so on fire when he returned to Kentucky that he walked up to a crowd of tough looking construction workers in a restaurant and fervently pleaded with them to give their lives to the Lord. The men were stunned. One wept openly.

Another thing that occurs when a person has been touched by the flames of the Holy Spirit is the process of refining. The closer a person draws to God, the more he will find the Lord searching his heart and dealing with him about the un-Christlike motives and attitudes lodged within his heart. Malachi predicted that the Messiah would be "like a refiner's fire and like fullers' soap." (Malachi 3:2b)

Malachi's illustrations perfectly describe how the Holy Spirit works to cleanse the polluting effects of sin within a person's heart. A believer can and should do his utmost to examine his inner being for sinful attitudes and so on, but ultimately he cannot purify his own heart. His efforts would be as hopeless as it would be for a potter to attempt to purge impurities out of a lump of clay with a hammer and chisel. Only the fire of a furnace will melt away the dross.

Spiritual fire has a way of separating wheat from chaff. Jesus said, "I have come to cast fire upon the earth; and how I wish it were already kindled! But I have a baptism to undergo, and how distressed I am until it is accomplished! Do you suppose that I came to grant peace on earth? I tell you, no, but rather division; for from now on five members in one household will be divided, three against two and two against three." (Luke 12:49-52)

I believe that the great revival we will witness in our day is going to deepen the rift between true believers and those who hold a spurious faith. Those who allow the Holy Spirit to have His way in their lives will become increasingly on fire. On the other hand, those who quench the fire of the Holy Spirit will become increasingly more calloused.

Any chemist will attest to the fact that fire does not cause the burning material to disappear. Fire is simply an agent that changes the molecular structure of the material which is burning. The reaction that occurs is completely determined by the substance it encounters. Put wax under a flame and it will melt, while a lump of clay sitting next to it will only harden. In the same way, the fire of God will cause some to melt in contrition, while others will grow more hard-hearted.

A lukewarm Church does little to arouse opposition. However, when men and women are stirred to live in a fervent love for souls; when their affections have been set ablaze and they begin preaching in the fire of the Holy Ghost, then those who don't want what is being offered will become enraged at them.

I believe this is one of the characteristics Jesus revealed about the end-times Church. In His discourse about the end-times, He said, "At that time many will fall away and will betray one another and hate one another." (Matthew 24:10) Since the context is professing Christians, we have to ask ourselves who are the betrayers and who are the betrayed?

THE FALL OF THE APOSTATE CHURCH

The book of Revelation seems to indicate that the world is going to turn against the Harlot Church before the End. (Revelation 17:16) They tolerated her because she did nothing to convict them of their sins. Now, her usefulness has come to an end and they hate her for her hypocrisy. False brethren will face persecution, but it will not be "for the sake of the Son of Man."

However, the greater downfall is the *spiritual* plunge she takes when she turns on the true Bride of Christ. The final aspect of the Great Apostasy occurs as unconverted evangelicals give vent to their anger against radical believers.

Of all of the astonishing things John saw in his vision, there was only one sight at which he "wondered greatly." It was when he saw that the harlot—the Apostate Church—had become "drunk with the blood of the saints, and with the blood of the witnesses of Jesus." (Revelation 17:6) John could understand persecution—he was a victim of it at that very time. What he could not fathom was that a time would come when professing Christians would actually be the chief persecutors against their brethren in the faith.

But Jesus had warned the disciples to expect this. One of the final things Jesus said was that, "…an hour is coming for everyone who kills you to think that he is offering service to God. These things they will do because they have not known the Father or Me." (John 16:2-3)

False believers have never repented of their rebellion against God's authority and never surrendered their wills to Him. As the lives of true saints expose their hypocrisy, they will turn against them with a fury. How could this be? George Bowen explains the inevitable clash between these two groups:

> The mission of Christians is to take from [a man] something that is unutterably dear to [him]…his own unblamableness. Every day of his life he has been engaged in rearing, in his inner thought-world, a lofty edifice…a monument in his own praise, and to enable him, when the time shall come, to step from its pinnacle into Heaven…
>
> You come to him in the name of Christ for the very purpose of depriving him of this idea of his own goodness. Your aim is to do what that tormenting

conscience of his, with all its advantages of time and place, failed to do. Do you think that he has fought with the Goliath of his own conscience so many times, and so successfully, to be now discomfited by you? Will he allow you to be victorious over him, and take from him the idea of his own integrity in the sight of God, after he has gone through a thousand fights to obtain that pearl of price?

You tell him that he is a mere rebel against the most high God, that he has never been anything else, that all his righteousnesses are contemptible in the sight of Heaven, that he deserves the wrath of God, and you ask him to take this same view of himself...Self-esteem permeates his whole nature like the fibers of a cancer, and to bid him part with it is like bidding him surrender life.[4]

Pseudo-Christians have built their entire spiritual lives upon the false foundation of their own worthiness. To acknowledge that the on-fire believers are right in their intimations would be tantamount to admitting that everything they have ever done in the name of Christ has been in vain. It would mean that they would have to renounce that which is their most prized possession: the belief in their own goodness. This is a concept they are unwilling to even entertain. They *must* silence the lips of the true saints. They are determined to serve their counterfeit Christianity to the very end.

Outwardly, it will seem that the Apostate Church is prevailing against the Remnant, but, as in the case of the First Century Jewish religion, it is the beginning of the end. Once professing Christians turn on real believers, the end will be in sight. Dear one, which side of the fence will you find yourself on when red-hot persecution breaks out against the saints of God?

There is a fire coming to this earth that will display itself in various ways. The final manifestation will be as an agent of destruction. If a person continues to quench, resist and grieve the Holy Spirit, he must ultimately face the fires of judgment. At one point Jesus explained to His followers: "If your eye causes you to stumble, throw it out; it is better for you to enter the kingdom of God with one eye, than, having two eyes, to be cast into hell, where their worm does not die, and the fire is not quenched. For everyone will be salted with fire." (Mark 9:47-49) In other words, it is better to allow God to cut the sin out of your heart now than to face the consequences of it in Judgment. Of this passage, Alexander MacLaren wrote:

> Jesus Christ did not exaggerate. If here and now sin has so destructive an effect upon a man, O, who will venture to say that he knows the limits of its murderous power in that future life, when retribution shall begin with new energy and under new conditions?
>
> Brethren, whilst I dare not enlarge, I still less dare to suppress; and I ask you to remember that not I, or any man, but Jesus Christ Himself, has put before each of us this alternative—either the fire unquenchable, which destroys a man, or the merciful fire, which slays his sins and saves him alive.[5]

"There is only one thing that promises less than it performs, and which can satisfy a man's soul; and that is cleaving to God. Go to Him, let nothing draw you away from Him. Let us hold by Him in love, thought, obedience; and the lies that tempt us to our destruction will have no power over us; and we shall possess joys that neither pall nor end." ❧Alexander MacLaren[1]

"To save one immortal soul from eternal death is worth the labor of a lifetime." ❧Alfred Plummer[2]

"If sinners be damned at least let them leap to hell over our bodies. If they will perish let them perish with our arms about their knees. Let no one go there unwarned and unprayed for."
❧Charles Spurgeon[3]

EPILOGUE

*"Rescue those being led away to death; hold back
those staggering toward slaughter. If you say, 'But we
knew nothing about this,' does not he who weighs the
heart perceive it? Does not he who guards your life
know it? Will he not repay each person according to
what he has done?"* (Proverbs 24:11-12 NIV)

My dear reader, can I ask you to please take a moment to consider two urgent matters?

First, are you absolutely certain that your salvation experience is genuine? I know you have been spiritually enlightened. I realize that you go to a Bible-believing church. I'm certain that you have had spiritual experiences—even felt the presence of God and seen Him at work in your life. But the consequences are too grave and there is too much at risk to rest your eternal destiny on such fleeting things as these.

Scripture gives clear-cut proofs of salvation. Honestly, prayerfully examine your life and humbly ask yourself these questions:

- Do you see the love of God flowing through your life, meeting the needs of others, or are you just a "nice person" living for yourself? *"We know that we have passed out of death into life, because we love the brethren. He who does not love abides in death."* (I John 3:14)

- Are you continually living in repentance, or are you involved in unrepentant sin? *"No one who abides in Him sins... Little children, make sure no one deceives you... the one who practices sin is of the devil..."* (I John 3:6-8)

- Are you certain you are doing the will of God, or are you just giving Him a corner of your life while doing your own thing? *"...he who does the will of My Father who is in heaven will enter."* (Matthew 7:21) *"...the one who does the will of God lives forever."* (I John 2:17)

- Is your life truly consecrated to God, or are you given over to the things of the world? *"You adulteresses, do you not know that friendship with the world is hostility toward God? Therefore whoever wishes to be a friend of the world makes himself an enemy of God."* (James 4:4)

- Is there really fruit coming from your life, or do you just occasionally do some religious deed to prop up a lifeless faith? *"...faith without works is dead."* (James 2:26)

- Do you love God with all your heart, soul and mind, or do you have idols in your life that deaden any affection you might have for Him? *"Now the deeds of the flesh are evident... idolatry... I have forewarned you, that those who practice such things will not inherit the kingdom of God."* (Galatians 5:19-21)

- If you are a minister, are you laying your life down for others, or are you just using the ministry for your own selfish purposes? *"Every tree that does not bear good fruit is cut down and thrown into the fire."* (Matthew 7:19)

You cannot earn your way into heaven by attempting to

implement these things into your life. But if you will, as a simple act of your will, give up your life to Christ, renounce everything displeasing to Him—no matter how much it may mean to you— and truly submit yourself to His authority, the Spirit of Christ will take up residence in your heart. If that really does happen, all of the "fruit" described above will soon become manifested in your life. Today, the door is open. The cry continues to go forth from the great Throne: "Whosoever will, come!"

The second matter of grave concern is that of the lost souls that surround you. No, better yet, consider only one of them. Take just a minute to focus your thoughts on one unsaved loved one in light of the terrible realities expressed in Chapter Seven. Think of that person screaming in horror as he discovers his eternal doom. I realize this is a very unpleasant thought, but this will happen if something doesn't change in his life. Ponder the other side of it. What would it be like to see that person in love with God? Consider the joy of walking hand-in-hand through Paradise together.

Could there possibly be anything that would hinder you from interceding with flowing tears and great passion for that person's soul? Is there any reason you wouldn't pray and even fast regularly for that loved one's salvation?

I realize that bringing a lost soul to a true conversion is no small matter. He has believed lies about God and his relationship to Him for many years. Throughout his entire life he has probably had a lying devil in his ears, paving a smooth path to hell through the use of flattery: "You're a good person. You don't need to be concerned about going to hell."

I also realize this person has a mountain of pride that must be brought low. He probably thinks he deserves to be in heaven. He doesn't believe he needs anyone's help to make it through life. He is quite confident in his abilities.

Undoubtedly, he also loves the temporary pleasures offered

by this fallen world. He doesn't realize the emptiness of this world and the futility of a life without Christ.

I can understand why this person's salvation would seem like an unconquerable mountain. But remember what Jesus said: "...if you have faith the size of a mustard seed, you will say to this mountain, 'Move from here to there,' and it will move; and nothing will be impossible to you." (Matthew 17:20) I have seen many mountains of unbelief vanish! God can do it!

There is an old adage that is worth noting: How do you eat an elephant? One bite at a time. That is the key to prevailing prayer for a lost soul. Every time you offer a heartfelt prayer on his behalf, in a very real way you are removing obstacles to his conversion. If the mountain seems too daunting for you, allow me to offer a piece of practical advice. For the next two weeks, spend 15 minutes every morning praying for that person's conversion. Also, during that span of time, fast for 24-hours, two separate times (e.g. eat lunch and then don't eat again until lunch the following day). After two weeks, ask the Lord if you should continue to pray for that person or move on to someone else. One way or another, this will establish a habit in your life and increase your confidence that God really is hearing your prayers.

Pray that the Holy Spirit will overthrow the lies of the enemy, humble the person, help him to see the futility of this world, grasp the shortness of life and comprehend the great love of God. Every morning plead this person's cause before the great Throne. Remember, you are going before a Judge who *wants* to grant your request! Ask, seek and keep knocking. Bombard heaven on this person's behalf every morning. Don't get discouraged if you don't see outward results right away. God works behind the scenes.

You must resist the temptation of attempting to accomplish in the flesh what can only happen in the Spirit. People of little faith typically try to talk the person into becoming a Christian. It nearly always does more harm than good, serving only to drive a wedge between them and the sinner. However, I must qualify this statement by saying that there may come a day when *you know* that the Lord has arranged the perfect situation for you to pour your heart out to this unbeliever. If it is the Lord's doing, there will probably be tears in your eyes!

Dear one, will you undertake for the lost souls the Lord has placed in your path? If you won't take up their cause, who will? If God can't count on you to stand in the gap for these doomed souls, who can He turn to? Won't you do your utmost to rescue them?

While it is true that winning a soul to Christ requires a great deal of effort, think of what is at stake! Is it any wonder that Jesus said that all heaven lights up in joy when a sinner repents? (Luke 15:7) There is no greater thing you or I could possibly do than to intercede for people on their way to hell. I will close with the following words of Richard Baxter:

> Go to poor sinners with tears in your eyes, that they may see you believe them to be miserable, and that you unfeignedly pity their case. Deal with them with earnest, humble entreaties. Let them perceive it is the desire of your heart to do them good; that you have no other end but their everlasting happiness; and that it is your sense of their danger, and your love to their souls, that forces you to speak; even because you "know the terrors of the Lord," and for fear you should see them in eternal torments.[3]

NOTES

CHAPTER ONE

1. Dietrich Bonhoeffer, *The Cost of Discipleship* (New York, NY: Collier Books, 1937) p. 99.
2. Thomas À Kempis, *The Imitation of Christ* (London, England: Vintage Publishers, 1998) p 73.
3. A.W. Tozer, *The Radical Cross* (Camp Hill, PA: Wingspread Publishers, 2006) p. 5.
4. Cecil B. Knight, *Inspiring Quotations* (Nashville, TN: Thomas Nelson Publishers, 1988) p. 178.
5. Mark Seager, Telegraph Company, U.K. News, October 12, 2000, accessed online at http://www.telegraph.co.uk/news/main.jhtml;jsessionid=55J4D4VU1G3TBQFIQMGCFFWAVCBQUIV0?xml=/news/2000/10/15/wmid315.xml.
6. Ofer Amitai, a Sermon delivered at Pure Life Ministries, Dry Ridge, Kentucky (1994).
7. Joni Eareckson Tada and Rev. Steven Estes, *When God Weeps* (Grand Rapids, MI: Zondervan, 1997) p. 53.
8. George Bowen, *Love Revealed* (London, England: M.O.V.E. Press, 1977 edition), p. 22.
9. *Ibid.*, p. 53.
10. Alexander MacLaren, *Perishing or Being Saved*, as cited in AGES Digitial Library (Rio, WI: AGES Software, Inc., 2001).

CHAPTER TWO

1. Martin Luther, as cited by Leonard Ravenhill in *Why Revival Tarries* (Minneapolis, MN: Bethany House Publishers, 1996) p. 122.
2. Leonard Ravenhill, from the Sermon "Repent, Repent, Repent" accessed online at http://www.ravenhill.org/mp3.htm.
3. Milton Green, *The Great Falling Away Today* (Palestine, TX: Be Fruitful and Multiply Ministries, 1994) p. 122.
4. Charles Spurgeon, *Spots in Our Feasts of Charity*, as cited in AGES Digital Library (Rio, WI: AGES Software, Inc., 2001).
5. Ray Comfort, *The Mantle of the Harlot: The Ultimate Deception* (Bellflower,

    CA: Living Waters Publications, 1992) p. 17.
6.   J.R. Thompson, *The Pulpit Commentary,* as cited in AGES Digital Library (Rio, WI: AGES Software, Inc., 2001) p. 15.
7.   Adam Clarke, *Clarke's Commentaries on the New Testament,* as cited in AGES Digital Library (Rio, WI: AGES Software, Inc., 2001) p. 279.
8.   Matthew Henry, *Commentary on the New Testament,* as cited in AGES Digital Library (Rio, WI: AGES Software, Inc., 2001) p. 47.
9.   Joel R. Beeke, "Signs of Backsliding Churches" *Free Grace Broadcaster,* (Fall 2006) p. 30.
10. B.C. Caffin, *The Pulpit Commentary,* as cited in AGES Digital Library (Rio, WI: AGES Software, Inc., 2001) p. 36.
11. Ray Comfort, p. 88.
12. Steve Gallagher, *Intoxicated with Babylon* (Dry Ridge, KY: Pure Life Ministries, 2006), p. 24.
13. *Ibid.*
14. *The 1912 Weymouth New Testament,* as cited in AGES Digital Library (Rio, WI: AGES Software, Inc., 2001) p. 167.
15. W.E. Vine, *Vine's Expository Dictionary of Old and New Testament Words* (Old Tappan, NJ: Fleming H. Revell Co., 1981) pps. 163 & 164.
16. Albert Barnes, *Notes on the Bible,* as cited in AGES Digital Library (Rio, WI: AGES Software, Inc., 2001) p. 291.
17. Matthew Henry, p. 432.
18. Adam Clarke, p. 281.
19. Charles Spurgeon, *A Popular Exposition to the Gospel According to Matthew,* as cited in AGES Digital Library (Rio, WI: AGES Software, Inc., 2001) p. 174.
20. Adam Clarke, p. 290.
21. A. Lukyn Williams, *The Pulpit Commentary,* as cited in AGES Digital Library (Rio, WI: AGES Software, Inc., 2001) p. 26.
22. Ray Comfort, p. 19.
23. George Bowen, p. 27.

CHAPTER THREE

1.   C.S. Lewis, *The Quotable Lewis* (Wheaton, IL: Tyndale House Publishers, 1989) p. 571.
2.   Soren Kierkegaard, *Topical Encyclopedia of Living Quotations* (Minneapolis, MN: Bethany House Publishers, 1982) p. 235.
3.   Matthew Henry, p. 311.
4.   E. Stanley Jones, *Conversion* (Nashville, TN: Abingdon Press, 1959) p. 53.
5.   George Bowen, p. 180.
6.   W.B. Godbey, *Commentary on the New Testament,* as cited in AGES Digital Library (Rio, WI: AGES Software, Inc. 2001) p. 12.
7.   E. Stanley Jones, pps. 55-56.

CHAPTER FOUR

1.   Milton Green, *The Great Falling Away Today,* p. 115.
2.   A.W. Tozer, *I Call it Heresy* (Camp Hill, PA: Wingspread Publishers, 2007) pps. 2-3.

3. Charles Finney, "Self Deceivers, Lectures to Professing Christians, delivered in New York City between 1836 and 1837. Accessed online at http://www.bibleteacher.org/finlec_a.htm#Ch1.

4. David S. Kirkwood, *The Great Gospel Deception: Exposing the False Promise of Heaven Without Holiness* (Pittsburgh, PA: Ethnos Press, 1999) p. 105.

5. *Ibid.,* p. 76.

6. John MacArthur, *The MacArthur New Testament Commentaries: Matthew 1-7* (Chicago, IL: Moody Bible Institute, 1985) pps. 474 - 475.

7. John Piper, *Letter to a Friend Concerning the So-Called 'Lordship Salvation'* (Pensacola, FL: Chapel Library Press, 1992), p. 7.

8. *Strong's Exhaustive Concordance of the Bible with Greek and Hebrew Dictionaries* (Grand Rapids, MI: Zondervan, 2001).

9. W.E. Vine, *Vine's Expository Dictionary* (Nashville, TN: Thomas Nelson, Inc., 1996).

10. David S. Kirkwood, p. 35.

11. John Dillenberger (Editor), *Martin Luther: Selections From His Writings* (Norwell, MA: Anchor Press, 1958) p. 24.

12. David S. Kirkwood, pps. 102-103.

13. *Ibid.,* p. 114.

CHAPTER FIVE

1. Charles Finney, *True and False Conversion* (Grand Rapids, MI: Alethea in Heart Ministries, 2002) p. 76.

2. Oswald Chambers, *Oswald Chambers: The Best from All His Books* (Nashville, TN: Thomas Nelson Publishers, 1987) pps. 16, 19.

3. J.C. Ryle, *Holiness* (Darlington, England: Evangelical Press, 1897) p. 22.

4. John MacArthur, pps. 454-455.

5. John Wesley, *The Works of John Wesley,* as cited in AGES Digital Library (Rio, WI: AGES Software, Inc. 2001) p. 483.

6. Charles Finney, *Lectures to Professing Christians,* as cited in AGES Digital Library (Rio, WI: AGES Software, Inc. 2001) p. 16.

7. Dr. Martyn Lloyd-Jones, *Studies in the Sermon on the Mount, second edition* (Grand Rapids, MI: Wm. B. Eerdmans Publishing Company, 1976), p. 535.

8. Ray Comfort, pps. 14-15.

9. John Wesley, p. 480.

CHAPTER SIX

1. William C. Nichols, *The Terrors of Hell* (Pensacola FL: Chapel Library Press, 1992), p. 7.

2. Charles Spurgeon, *Sermons: 250 Selected Expositions,* as cited in AGES Digital Library (Rio, WI: AGES Software, Inc. 2001) p. 169.

3. John Bunyan, *Bunyan's Practical Works,* as cited in AGES Digital Library (Rio, WI: AGES Software, Inc. 2001) p. 329.

4. Dr. W.E. Sangster, as cited by Leonard Ravenhill in *Why Revival Tarries* (Minneapolis, MN: Bethany House Publishers, 1996) p. 70.

5. Charles Finney, *God's Anger Against the Wicked,* as cited in AGES Digital Library (Rio, WI: AGES Software, Inc. 2001) p. 558.
6. George G. Ritchie and Elizabeth Sherrill, *Return from Tomorrow* (Grand Rapids, MI: Revell, 1995) pps. 52 - 53.
7. Adam Clarke, p. 246.

CHAPTER SEVEN

1. John Trapp, *The Biblical Illustrator,* Matthew 24, as cited in AGES Digital Library (Rio, WI: AGES Software Inc., 2001).
2. Glenn Meldrum, *Destiny of the Damned* (Milton, FL: In His Presence Ministries) pps. 12, 18, 26.
3. Charles Spurgeon, *The Best of C.H. Spurgeon* (Grand Rapids, MI: Baker Book House, 1986) p. 23.
4. C.S. Lewis, p. 292.
5. Jonathan Edwards, *The Works of Jonathan Edwards,* as cited in AGES Digital Library (Rio, WI: AGES Software, Inc., 2001) p. 1420.
6. Albert Barnes, p. 195.
7. John Bunyan, *Visions of Heaven & Hell* (New Kensington, PA: Whitaker House, 1998) pps. 125-126.
8. *Ibid.,* pps. 139-140.
9. Charles Finney, *The Wages of Sin,* as cited in AGES Digital Library (Rio, WI: AGES Software, Inc. 2001) p. 1101.

CHAPTER EIGHT

1. R. Hall, *Biblical Illustrator, II Corinthians 11,* as cited in AGES Digital Library (Rio, WI: AGES Software Inc., 2001).
2. A.W. Tozer, as cited by Leonard Ravenhill in *Why Revival Tarries,* p. 76.
3. Leonard Ravenhill, *America is Too Young to Die* (Minneapolis, MN: Bethany House Publishers, 1979) p. 52.
4. Matthew Henry, *Matthew Henry's Commentary on the Whole Bible* (Peabody, MA: Hendrickson Publishers, Inc., 1991) p. 643.
5. Albert Barnes, *Notes on the Bible,* as cited in AGES Digital Library (Rio, WI: AGES Software, Inc., 2001) p. 805.
6. T. Croskery, as quoted in *The Pulpit Commentary,* as cited in AGES Digital Library (Rio, WI: AGES Software, Inc., 2001) p. 14.
7. John Owen, *Sermons, II Timothy 3,* as cited in AGES Digital Library (Rio, WI: AGES Software, Inc., 2001).
8. *Ibid.*
9. *Ibid.*

CHAPTER NINE

1. E. Stanley Jones, p. 59.
2. Leonard Ravenhill, *America is Too Young to Die,* p. 74.
3. Rex Andrews, *What the Bible Teaches About Mercy* (Zion, IL: Zion Faith Homes, 1985), p. 197.
4. A.W. Pink, *The Cross and Self* (Pensacola, FL: Chapel Library Press).
5. C.S. Lewis, pps. 403, 410.

CHAPTER TEN

1. Jamieson Faussett Brown, *Commentary on the New Testament,* as cited in AGES Digital Library (Rio, WI: AGES Software, Inc., 2001) p. 1664.
2. Joel R. Beeke, pps. 29 & 30.
3. E. Payson, *Biblical Illustrator, Acts 3,* as cited in AGES Digital Library (Rio, WI: AGES Software Inc., 2001).
4. Jack W. Plunkett, *Plunkett's Entertainment & Media Industry Almanac 2006* (Houston, TX: Plunkett Research, Ltd., 2006).
5. The Henry J. Kaiser Family Foundation, *Sex on TV 4,* (2005), accessed at http://www.kff.org/entmedia/entmedia110905pkg.cfm.
6. Parents Television Council Publications, *Facts and TV Statistics,* accessed at http://www.parentstv.org/PTC/facts/mediafacts.asp.
7. *Ibid.*
8. *Ibid.*
9. *Ibid.*
10. *Ibid.*
11. Steve Gallagher, *Intoxicated With Babylon,* pps. 26-27.

CHAPTER ELEVEN

1. Thomas Trask, as quoted in *The Council Today,* August 9, 2007.
2. C. Clemance, *The Pulpit Commentary,* as cited in AGES Digital Library (Rio, WI: AGES Software, Inc., 2001) p. 34.
3. Joseph Henry Thayer, *Thayer's Greek-English Lexicon of the New Testament* (Peabody, MA: Hendrickson Publishers, Inc., 1996).
4. *Webster's New World Dictionary of the American Language* (Cleveland, OH: The World Publishing Company, 1962).
5. Joseph Henry Thayer.
6. J.C. Ryle, p. 7.
7. Aaron Merritt Hills, *Mocking At Sin,* as cited in AGES Digital Library (Rio, WI: AGES Software, Inc., 2001).
8. Steve Gallagher, *How America Lost Her Innocence* (Dry Ridge, KY: Pure Life Ministries, 2005) pps. 90-92.

CHAPTER TWELVE

1. Matthew Henry, p. 697.
2. J.C. Ryle, p. 18.
3. Samuel Chadwick, as cited by Leonard Ravenhill in *Why Revival Tarries,* p. 28.

CHAPTER THIRTEEN

1. Alexander MacLaren, *Form and Power,* as cited in AGES Digital Library (Rio, WI: AGES Software, Inc., 2001).
2. Leonard Ravenhill, *Meat for Men* (Minneapolis, MN: Bethany House Publishers, 1961) p. 97.
3. Steve Gallagher, *Intoxicated with Babylon,* p. 104.

CHAPTER FOURTEEN

1. W.F. Adeney, *Pulpit Commentary, Jeremiah 1,* as cited in AGES Digital

Library (Rio, WI: AGES Software, Inc., 2001), p. 8.

2. Thomas À Kempis, p. 69.
3. John Wesley, p. 486.
4. Os Guiness, *Dining with the Devil* (Grand Rapids, MI: Baker Books, 2001) p. 24.
5. Berit Kjos, *Spirit-Led or Purpose-Driven?*, November 2003, accessed at http://www.crossroad.to/articles2/2003/1-purpose.htm#word.
6. Ron Auch, Dean Niforatos, *The Jesus Sensitive Church* (Green Forest, AR: New Leaf Press, 2006) p. 43.
7. George Barna, www.barna.org, unknown date. However, for a more recent evaluation, see: http://www.barna.org/FlexPage.aspx?Page=B arnaUpdate&BarnaUpdateID=235.
8. Jackie Alnor, *Prosperity Gospel's Coverboy,* accessed at http://www.cultlink.com.
9. Dr. Terry Watkins, accessed at www.av1611.org.
10. *Ibid.*
11. David Wilkerson, "When Men Cry Peace and Safety" *World Challenge Pulpit Series,* December 2006.
12. Adam Clarke, p. 453.

CHAPTER FIFTEEN

1. Charles Finney, as printed in *The Oberlin Evangelist,* February 12, 1840, accessed online at http://www.gospeltruth.net/1840OE/40%20lets_art/400212_ministers_1.htm.
2. Charles Spurgeon, *Spots in Our Feasts of Charity.*
3. W.F. Adeney, *Pulpit Commentary, Lamentations 3,* as cited in AGES Digital Library (Rio, WI: AGES Software, Inc., 2001), p. 14.
4. Rita Healy/Denver, "A Mega-Scandal for a Mega-Church" *Time,* November 03, 2006.

CHAPTER SIXTEEN

1. George Bowen, p. 79.
2. Charles Spurgeon, *The Marriage Supper of the Lamb,* as cited in AGES Digital Library (Rio, WI: AGES Software, Inc., 2001).
3. Jim and Merry Corbett, *From Our Father's Heart to You* (Pittsburgh, PA: Hartline Marketing, 2001), p. 210.
4. Glenn Meldrum, *Rend the Heavens* (Covert, MI: In His Presence Ministries, 2004) p. 20.
5. Charles Finney, *The Autobiography of Charles Finney* (Minneapolis, MN: Bethany House Publishing, 1977), p. 57.
6. *Ibid.,* p. 75.
7. *Ibid.,* p. 28.
8. Young-Hoon Lee, as quoted by Glenn Meldrum in *Rend the Heavens,* p. 154.
9. *Floods on Dry Land,* compiled and edited by Jessica Meldrum (Covert, MI: In His Presence Ministries, 2004), p. 15.
10. Steve Gallagher, *Out of the Depths of Sexual Sin,* (Dry Ridge, KY: Pure Life Ministries, 2004) p. 183.

11. Jim and Merry Corbett, pps. 248-249.

CHAPTER SEVENTEEN

1. Samuel Chadwick, as cited by Leonard Ravenhill in *Why Revival Tarries*, p. 100.
2. Milton Green, pps. 119, 204.
3. Sir Robert Anderson, *The Lord from Heaven*, as cited in AGES Digital Library (Rio, WI: AGES Software, Inc., 2001), p. 57.
4. George Bowen, pps. 143-144.
5. Alexander MacLaren, *Salted with Fire*, as cited in AGES Digital Library (Rio, WI: AGES Software, Inc., 2001).

EPILOGUE

1. Alexander MacLaren, *The Lies of the Temptress*, as cited in AGES Digital Library (Rio, WI: AGES Software, Inc., 2001).
2. Alfred Plummer, *Expositor's Bible*, as cited in AGES Digital Library (Rio, WI: AGES Software, Inc., 2001).
3. Richard Baxter, *The Saint's Everlasting Rest*, as cited in AGES Digital Library (Rio, WI: AGES Software, Inc., 2001).

INTOXICATED WITH BABYLON

Intoxicated with Babylon is by far Steve Gallagher's best writing; its strength is his sobering deliverance of the unvarnished truth to a Church rife with sensuality and worldly compromise. In a time when evangelical Christians seem content to be lulled to sleep by the spirit of Antichrist, *Intoxicated with Babylon* sounds a clarion wake-up call in an effort to draw the Body of Christ back to the Cross and holy living. Those with itching ears will find no solace here, but sincere believers will experience deep repentance and a fresh encounter with the Living God.

IRRESISTIBLE TO GOD

Before a person can come into intimate contact with a Holy God, he must first be purged of the hideous cancer of pride that lurks deep within his heart.

"This book is a road map that shows the arduous but rewarding way out of the pit of pride and into the green pastures of humility. Here is the place of blessing and favor with God."—Steve Gallagher

Humility is the key that opens the door into the inner regions of intimacy with God. *Irresistible to God* unfolds the mystery that God is indeed drawn to the one who is crushed in spirit, broken by his sin, and meek before the Lord and others.

AT THE ALTAR OF SEXUAL IDOLATRY

The most comprehensive book on habitual sexual sin available today! Sexual temptation is undeniably the greatest struggle Christian men face. Here's a book that digs deep and has the answers men are looking for—the kind that actually work. While other books deal with the subject superficially, *At the Altar of Sexual Idolatry* goes right to the heart. Put an end to the mystery of lust and maximize God's power in your life with the proven answers that have helped thousands.

WHEN HIS SECRET SIN BREAKS YOUR HEART

What can be more devastating for a wife than to discover her husband has a secret obsession with pornography and other women? Yet, this is what countless Christian wives face every day. Kathy Gallagher has been there; she understands the pain of rejection, the feelings of hopelessness and the questions that plague a hurting wife. In this collection of letters, Kathy imparts heart-felt encouragement by providing the practical, biblical answers that helped her find healing in the midst of her most trying storm. The 30-day journal offers wives a place to prayerfully reflect and meditate upon Kathy's letters.

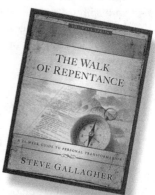
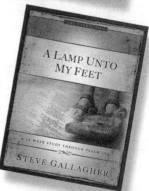

PURE LIFE MINISTRIES

Pure Life Ministries helps Christian men achieve lasting freedom from sexual sin. The Apostle Paul said, "Walk in the Spirit and you will not fulfill the lust of the flesh." Since 1986, Pure Life Ministries (PLM) has been discipling men into the holiness and purity of heart that comes from a Spirit-controlled life. At the root, illicit sexual behavior is sin and must be treated with spiritual remedies. Our counseling programs and teaching materials are rooted in the biblical principles that, when applied to the believer's daily life, will lead him out of bondage and into freedom in Christ.

BIBLICAL TEACHING MATERIALS

Pure Life offers a full line of books, audiotapes and videotapes specifically designed to give men the tools they need to live in sexual purity.

RESIDENTIAL CARE

The most intense and involved counseling PLM offers comes through the **Live-in Program** (6-12 months), in Dry Ridge, Kentucky. The godly and sober atmosphere on our 45-acre campus provokes the hunger for God and deep repentance that destroys the hold of sin in men's lives.

HELP AT HOME

The **Overcomers At Home Program** (OCAH) is available for those who cannot come to Kentucky for the Live-in program. This twelve-week counseling program features weekly counseling sessions and many of the same teachings offered in the Live-in Program.

CARE FOR WIVES

Pure Life Ministries also offers help to wives of men in sexual sin. Our wives' counselors have suffered through the trials and storms of such a discovery and can offer a devastated wife a sympathetic ear and the biblical solutions that worked in their lives.

PURE LIFE MINISTRIES
14 School St. • Dry Ridge • KY • 41035
Office: 859.824.4444 • Orders: 888.293.8714
info@purelifeministries.org
www.purelifeministries.org